ALL-AMERICAN
★ ★ ★ ★

LOW·FAT
MEALS
IN MINUTES

RECIPES AND MENUS

FOR SPECIAL OCCASIONS

OR EVERY DAY

M.J. SMITH
MA, RD, LD

All-American Low-Fat Meals in Minutes. ©1990 by DCI Publishing, I

Library of Congress Cataloging-in-Publication Data
Smith, M.J. (Margaret Jane), 1955-
  All-American low-fat meals in minutes: recipes & menus for spec
occasions or everyday/M.J. Smith
    p.   cm.
  Includes index.
  ISBN 0-937721-73-5 : $12.95
RM237.7.S59   1990   90-21955
641.5'638--dc20

Edited by: Donna Hoel
Cover & Text Design: Terry Dugan
Art/Production Manager: Wenda Johnson
Printed in the United States of America

10 9 8 7 6 5 4 3 2 1

Published by:
DCI Publishing, Inc.
P.O. Box 47945
Minneapolis, MN 55447-9727

Table of Contents

FOREWORD

★ ★ ★

O verheard in the dietitian's office . . .
"I'm so tired of chicken breasts!"
"Can't you give me some menus for this diet?"
"What am I going to take to the potluck?"
"I understand cholesterol, but what about other fats?"
"My cholesterol is too high, but my husband and family love good
food."

Lowering fat is a major nutrition goal for the U.S., but it's easy to
be confused about how to do it. This book was written to help
people translate a low-fat diet into interesting menus and good
food. Even if you don't have a weight or cholesterol problem, a
low-fat diet is nutrition insurance—one of the best prescriptions
for good health.

For ten years I have been helping people modify their family's
favorite casseroles and plan birthday parties without butter
creme frosting. Each of the 253 recipes in this book has been
thoughtfully developed using common ingredients, and most
require less than 30 minutes to prepare. My family and friends
have served as official taste testers, and they have enjoyed the
job.

This cookbook is unique because it includes downright tasty
menus and recipes for all seasons and many special occasions. By
using the menus with their corresponding recipes, you can control
fat and calories in an enjoyable way.

M.J. Smith, M.A., R.D., L.D.
Registered Dietitian

ACKNOWLEDGEMENTS

★ ★ ★

Thanks to my mother, Mary Agnes Budweg Rewoldt, for teaching me how to cook; to my husband Dr. Andrew Smith; and to my friends for their research and review of this book. It is dedicated to the hundreds of clients who have shared questions and frustrations and who have made my work fun.

INTRODUCTION

★ ★ ★

N early everyone is trying to control fat. Whether you're trying to lose weight, lower cholesterol, manage a health problem, or simply take good care of your body, a low-fat diet is important.

The National Cancer Institute recommends a low-fat diet to decrease the risk of cancers of the colon, breast, and prostate. As a dietitian, I have found that changing to a low-fat eating style is easier if you get the bottom line on "why?"

To help you get off to a good start, this book will tell you how a low-fat diet works. It also will give you information on finding low-fat foods at the supermarket and choosing healthy snacks.

LOWERING BLOOD CHOLESTEROL

★ ★ ★

C holesterol, a fatty, waxy, soapy substance that circulates in the blood, is a necessary part of the human body. It's a precursor, or beginning form, of many hormones. It's also involved in the formation of bile acids, which are needed for digestion. Cholesterol is widely distributed through the body and is an essential component of all cell membranes. So why is it a problem?

An important fact not often appreciated is that your body produces its own cholesterol in the liver. Even if you ate no cholesterol, your body would make an adequate supply. It's when you take in more than you can use that the trouble starts.

Too much cholesterol in the blood can lead to clogging of arteries and veins, a disease known as atherosclerosis. The problem begins when cholesterol becomes too concentrated in the blood and starts precipitating out. It's much like trying to stir a cup of salt into a cup of water. The salt is too concentrated and ends up collecting at the bottom of the glass.

When cholesterol is too concentrated in the blood, it is deposited on the sides of arteries and veins. Minerals, such as calcium, are then attracted to the affected areas. These minerals form a hard "plaque" that narrows the blood vessel, reduces its flexibility, and slows blood flow. Heart attack and stroke can follow.

Physicians use the following range to define blood cholesterol risks:

> -Less than 200 milligrams percent (often written *mg. %*) is low risk
> -200 to 240 mg. % is borderline high risk
> -More than 240 mg. % is high risk

If your blood cholesterol is over 200 mg. %, a diet low in fat and cholesterol is the first recommended treatment.

RECOGNIZING THE CULPRITS
★ ★ ★

C holesterol is found only in animal foods. We get it from eggs, whole-milk products, and fatty meats. To reduce the amount of circulating cholesterol, we need to cut down on these foods.

The American Heart Association recommends eating no more than 300 mg. of cholesterol daily. The following list shows the amount of cholesterol in common foods.

CHOLESTEROL CONTENT OF FOOD

Food Source	Serving Size	Cholesterol(mg.)
Whole milk	1 c.	33
2% milk	1 c.	18
Skim milk	1 c.	5
Low-fat yogurt	1 c.	14
Nonfat yogurt	1 c.	4
Creamy cottage cheese	1 c.	31
Low-fat cottage cheese	1 c.	19
Cheddar cheese	1 oz.	30
Part-skim mozzarella cheese	1 oz.	15
American cheese	1 oz.	27
Ice cream	1/2 c.	30
Ice milk	1/2 c.	9
Lean cooked beef arm roast	2 oz.	77
Lean cooked pork rib	3 oz.	67
Lean cooked skinless chicken	3 oz.	75
Halibut fillet, broiled	3 oz.	48
Crab legs, steamed	2 medium	96
Large egg	1	213
Butter	1 tsp.	10
Mayonnaise	1 tsp.	3
Sour cream	1 TB.	5
Light cream	1 TB.	10
Cream cheese	1 oz.	31

Nutrient values are from the American Dietetic Association, Manual of Clinical Dietetics, Chicago: American Dietetic Association, 1989; Pennington, Jean, and Church, Helen, Food Values, New York: Harper and Row, 1980; and United States Department of Agriculture, Cholesterol Content of Eggs, 1989.

While limiting animal cholesterol is important, restricting saturated fat and total fat in the diet is equally or perhaps more important. This is because saturated fat signals our own cells to make cholesterol and acts as the raw material for its manufacture. This is a concept that has been slow to be understood.

What is saturated fat? Well, it comes from animal and vegetable sources and it's usually hard at room temperature. Saturated fat is primarily found in:

> Visible or marbled fat in beef, veal, lamb, and pork
> Poultry skin and fat
> Butter, cream, and whole milk
> Products made from cream and whole milk,
>   such as cheese and ice cream
> Solid shortening
> Coconut oil
> Cocoa butter
> Palm and palm kernel oil
> Hydrogenated fats and oils. (These are oils that are
>   changed from their natural liquid form to become
>   more solid.)

It's a good idea to avoid these saturated fats as much as possible. The American Heart Association advises that no more than 10% of total calories come from saturated sources. Instead, polyunsaturated and mono-unsaturated fats should be used.

USING RATIOS

★ ★ ★

A nother way of evaluating fats involves the polyunsaturated-to-saturated (P/S) fat ratio.

To illustrate, we can look at the following nutrient label.

Mazola Light Corn Oil Spread

NUTRITION INFORMATION PER SERVING	
SERVING SIZE	1 TB.
SERVINGS PER CONTAINER (1 POUND)	32
CALORIES	50
PROTEIN	0 gm.
CARBOHYDRATE	0 gm.
FAT	6 gm.
POLYUNSATURATED FAT	2 gm.
SATURATED FAT	1 gm.

Notice the P/S ratio in this food is 2-to-1. This is preferred. If the ratio is less than 2-to-1, the food has more saturated fat than desirable.

POCKET GUIDE TO FAT GRAMS

★ ★ ★

T he following guide can be used for estimating intake of fat.
Numbers reflect averages for the food group.

Food   *Fat (grams)*

Non-fat beverages, 1-cup serving, including   0
coffee, tea, mineral water, fruit juices,
fruit drinks, tomato and vegetable juice,
and sugar-free soft drinks

All fruits, 1/2-cup serving, except avocado   0
(30 gm. in each)

Lean vegetables, 1-cup serving, including   0
asparagus, beets, broccoli, carrots, cauliflower,
celery, cabbage, cucumber, eggplant, green or
yellow beans, lettuce, mushrooms, onions,
peas, radishes, Brussels sprouts, kohlrabi,
leeks, okra, pea pods, spinach, sauerkraut,
zucchini, and water chestnuts

Starchy vegetables, 1/2-cup serving, including   0
potatoes, corn, squash, baked beans, lima
beans, sweet potatoes, and yams

Food	Fat (grams)
Dairy Products	
2% milk, 1 cup	5
1% milk, 1 cup	3
Skim or nonfat milk, 1 cup	1
Low-fat cottage cheese, 1/2 cup	3
Nonfat cottage cheese, 1/2 cup	1
American cheese, 1 oz.	9
Cheddar cheese, 1 oz.	9
Swiss cheese, 1 oz.	8
Light American cheese, 1 oz.	2
Light-Line® cheddar cheese, 1 oz.	2
Ice cream, 1/2 cup	7
Sherbet, 1/2 cup	0
Ice milk, 1/2 cup	3
Sorbet, 1/2 cup	0
Frozen yogurt, 1/2 cup	3
Grains and Cereals, including	1
1/2 c. any cereal without nuts	
1/2 c. rice or pasta	
1 slice bread, bun, English muffin, or bagel	
4 soda crackers or Rye-Crisps®	
1 oz. pretzels or breadsticks	
1 molasses cookie or 1 slice angel food cake	
2 vanilla wafers	
Meats, 1-oz. cooked serving	
Skinless white poultry	1
Skinless dark poultry	2
Fish, any white fish or tuna	1
Lean trimmed beef, including chuck, flank, rib- eye, round, lean ground beef, top loin, T-bone	4
Lean trimmed pork, including chop, loin, or shoulder or very lean ham	4

Food	Fat (grams)
Fats and Oils	
1 tsp. hard margarines or vegetable oil	5
2 tsp. mayonnaise or peanut butter	5
2 tsp. "diet" margarines	5
1 Tb. seeds or nuts	5

Add your favorite foods:

_____

_____

_____

My fat allowance is_____grams daily.

HOW MANY OF YOUR CALORIES COME FROM FAT?

★ ★ ★

A s we mentioned earlier, saturated fat and the total amount of fat we eat each day affect blood cholesterol levels. When we eat too much fat, our own body's production of cholesterol increases. That's why it's important to think about percentage of calories from fat.

Calories come from carbohydrates, protein, fat, and alcohol.

- 1 gram of carbohydrate has 4 calories
- 1 gram of protein has 4 calories
- 1 gram of fat has 9 calories
- 1 gram of alcohol has 7 calories

We can use a food example to show what this means.

One slice of French bread has 15 grams of carbohydrate and 2 grams of protein. One teaspoon of margarine has 5 grams of fat. From the slice of bread, we get 68 calories, and from the margarine we get 45 calories.

And now for the important part. *Zero percent* of the calories in French bread are from fat. *One hundred percent* of the calories in margarine are from fat. When we combine the bread with the margarine, we take in a total of 113 calories. Forty percent of these calories now come from fat.

To help control blood cholesterol, most of us should restrict the calories coming from fat to 30% or less of the total calories. And only 10% of the total should come from saturated fats.

(As we said earlier, saturated fats are found in regular cheeses, whole milk and cream, fatty beef, pork, lamb and poultry skin, coconut, palm kernel and palm oil. These fats are solid at room temperature.)

Here's an example of a dinner menu.

MENU A LA FAT

6 oz. Prime Rib
1 Baked Potato
1 Teaspoon Margarine
1/2 Cup Cauliflower Au Gratin
1 Cup Fresh Greens with 2 Tablespoons Salad Dressing
1 Cup Strawberries
1/2 Cup Ice Cream
Coffee

Total Calories: 987
Carbohydrate: 50 gm., or 200 calories, 20% of total
Protein: 46 gm., or 184 calories, 19% of total
Fat: 67 gm., or 603 calories, 61% of total

MENU A LA LEAN

3 oz. Sirloin
1 Baked Potato
1 Tablespoon Yogurt with Chives for Potato
1 Cup Steamed Cauliflower
1 Cup Fresh Greens with 1 Tablespoon No-Oil Dressing
1 Cup Strawberries
1/2 Cup Ice Milk
Coffee

Total Calories: 424
Carbohydrate: 55 gm. or 220 calories, 52% of total
Protein: 24 gm., or 96 calories, 23% of total
Fat: 12 gm., or 108 calories, 25% of total

Notice the simple changes that were made to reduce the fat from
61% to 25% of the total calories. The 6-oz. prime rib was changed
to a 3-oz. sirloin. Yogurt and chives were used to dress up the
potato instead of margarine. The cheese sauce was left off the

cauliflower. The salad dressing was made with no oil, and ice milk was used instead of ice cream.

The menus and recipes in this book are designed in a similar fashion—to keep the percentage of calories from fat at 30% or less and the percentage of calories from saturated fat at no more than 10%.

TWO WAYS TO CONTROL FAT

★ ★ ★

My patients have found two approaches that work to control total and saturated fat. The first involves liberal consumption of lean foods (fruits, vegetables, grains, skim-milk products), portion control of lean meats and unsaturated fats and oils, and avoiding saturated fats.

To review, the saturated fats are those visible on or marbled in red meat, poultry skin, butter, cream, and whole milk, products made from cream and whole milk, solid shortening, coconut oil, cocoa butter, palm and palm kernel oil, and hydrogenated fats.

This first approach is what I call the Low-Fat List, and it's very easy to understand. Once you're familiar with the list, you're home free.

This Low-Fat List is similar to the American Heart Association Diet, An Eating Plan for Healthy Americans.

LOW-FAT LIST

EAT   *AVOID*

Fruits and Vegetables

All in liberal amounts,   Olives, avocado, and coconut
   except those noted   Palm, coconut, and palm
                               kernel oils

Milk Products

Skim and 1% milk   Whole and 2% milk, cream
Any food made from   cheese with more than 2
   skim or 1% milk   grams of fat per ounce
Cheese with 2 grams   Nondairy creamers
   or less of fat per ounce   Regular and low-fat cottage
Nonfat cottage cheese   cheese and yogurt
Nonfat yogurt

Breads and Cereals

Plain breads and rolls   Egg, butter or cheese-rich
Low-fat crackers   breads
Pretzels, breadsticks   Party crackers
Popcorn   Potato and snack chips
Cereals   Mixes for cakes,
Rice and pasta   breads, or cookies
Starchy vegetables   Rice and pasta mixes
Broth or skim-milk   with added fat
   based soups   Chunky soups

EAT   *AVOID*

Meat, Fish, Poultry, Proteins

Skinless chicken and turkey	All poultry skin
Trimmed red meats	Duck, goose
85% lean ground beef	Prime red meats
Packaged sandwich meats with 2 grams or less of fat per ounce	Regular ground beef
Most fish	Pastrami, ribs
Dried beans, peas, legumes	Rib-eye cuts, hot dogs
Egg whites	Sausage, bacon
Wild game	Luncheon meats
	Bratwurst
	Organ meats

Limit all meat to 3 ounces per meal (about the size of a deck of cards).

Fats and Oils

Limit intake of the following oils to 1 or 2 teaspoons per meal:

Canola or Rapeseed	All solid fats and shortenings
Safflower	Butter
Corn	Bacon fat
Soybean	Ham hocks
Cottonseed	Meat fat
Sesame	Margarines not made from approved sources
Olive	Chocolate
Stick, tub, or squeeze margarines made from those oils	Coconut
Salad dressing made from those oils	Coconut oil
Low-calorie salad dressings	Palm oil
Peanut butter	Palm kernel oil
Seeds and nuts in 1 TB. servings	

COUNTING GRAMS OF FAT

★ ★ ★

T he second method for controlling fat in the diet involves writing down everything you eat and counting the fat in grams from those foods.

If you turn to the Pocket Guide to Fat Grams on page 8, you'll see that the grams of fat in fruits, vegetables, skim-milk products, and grains are very low. In contrast, the fat in red meats, margarines, and oils adds up quickly.

To count grams of fat from processed and prepared foods, you need a food counter book. I recommend Corrine Netzer's *The Complete Book of Food Counts*. It is available for $6.95 (including shipping) from Dell Readers' Service, Department DCN, P.O. Box 5057, Des Plaines Illinois, 60017. Ask for order number 20062-8. This book lists plain foods as well as name-brand processed and prepared foods in common serving sizes.

I have included a breakdown of fat content for all the menus and recipes in this book. At the risk of repeating myself for the fifth time, I'll just say avoid any fat you can see on meat or poultry, feel on sandwich meats or rich pastries, or smell on other tempting foods (and that includes butter, coconut oil, cocoa butter, palm and palm kernel oils, cream, and foods made with whole milk, solid shortening, and hydrogenated fats).

Now to the practical stuff. If you want to lower your cholesterol but you don't necessarily need to lose weight, you can use these guidelines.

For normal weight women, limit fat
to between 40 and 45 grams daily.

For normal weight men, limit fat
to between 50 and 60 grams daily.

To help you keep track, you can use the form that follows:

Keeping Track of Fat Grams   **Date**

Food/Amount   Fat, grams   Calories

Totals: _____   _____

My fat allowance is_____grams daily.

To calculate the percentage of calories from fat, multiply grams of fat by 9, then divide by the total calories.

Keeping Track of Fat Grams   **Date**

Food/Amount   Fat, grams   Calories

Totals: _____   _____

My fat allowance is_____grams daily.

To calculate the percentage of calories from fat, multiply grams of fat by 9, then divide by the total calories.

WEIGHT LOSS ON A LOW-FAT DIET

★ ★ ★

For the past three decades, dietitians have focused mostly on restricting calories to promote weight loss. Research is now showing us we use fat calories differently from carbohydrate or protein calories.

The body tends to use calories from fats more efficiently than those from carbohydrate and protein. At first that might sound like a good deal—more miles to the gallon, so to speak. But it's only good when you're going extra miles.

For every 100 calories of carbohydrate we eat, we may burn up 25 just processing (or metabolizing) that food energy. On the other hand, we only use about 5 of every 100 calories of fat in processing that fat. For anyone trying to lose weight, that makes a big difference.

When I have a patient interested in gradual weight loss, I start them out counting grams of fat. In many cases, this, combined with exercise, is all it takes to promote a gradual weight loss of one pound per week.

These are the guidelines I use to promote weight loss by counting grams of fat:

For women to lose weight, limit fat
to between 30 and 35 grams daily.

For men to lose weight, limit fat
to between 45 and 50 grams daily.

A hidden benefit of this system is that it promotes long-term habit changes. The weight loss is gradual and allows a person to learn a new way of eating.

Three main concepts are involved:
- Eat liberally from the fruit, vegetable, grain, and skim-milk food groups.
- Avoid saturated fats.
- Watch the portion sizes on lean meats and unsaturated fats.

In addition, you need to think about three other factors:

1. Exercise is mandatory. That is, to lose pounds and maintain a healthy weight over the long term, some regular form of exercise is necessary. The reason is simple. By elevating your heart rate during exercise, such as brisk walking, biking, swimming, dancing, or jogging, you burn calories faster. And that faster burn continues for one to three hours after you've stopped exercising. Also, exercise helps build and maintain muscle, and muscle uses more calories for energy than fat does.

2. Eat when you're going to work it off. Too many people save most of their fat allowance for the evening meal. Unless you take a brisk walk or perform some type of exercise in the evening, it's unlikely that those calories will be used for work. Instead, try to eat at least half your fat allowance before 2 p.m.

3. Consider smaller amounts of food eaten more often. We live in a society that loves grazing. And there is an advantage to this style for the low-fat dieter. Think about how you feel after a deep-fried meal that ends with cheesecake for dessert. You don't feel hungry for a long time. This is because the fat food remains in the digestive system longer than carbohydrate and protein and produces a feeling of fullness.

A low-fat dieter experiences hunger more quickly than before. That's why it is important to plan three light meals and two snacks daily. The frequent smaller meals ensure that you won't get a headache from being truly hungry and that you will be eating the food when you're going to use it for activity. The secret here is the word "planned." Snacks must be planned for, and I have included a section entitled A Low-Fat Snack for Every Tastebud to help you get started.

IF YOU'RE USING FOOD EXCHANGES

★ ★ ★

T he concept of using food groups to control calories and fat is common for several weight loss programs, including Weight Watchers. Diabetic diets also use an exchange system to promote weight loss and to control blood sugar. While there are some minor differences in various exchange plans, the principle is the same: You control total calories and fat by choosing foods from food groups in specific portion sizes.

Foods are divided into six groups. Each group represents foods of similar nutrient value. Calories and fat are controlled by carefully observing portion size.

The six groups are:
    Starch/Bread
    Meat
    Vegetables
    Fruit
    Milk
    Fat

The following pages list foods for each of the exchange groups, plus free and combination foods. Free foods are those with less than 20 calories per serving. Combination foods are those that represent more than one exchange group.

Each recipe in this book includes the exchange values, and the monthly menus fit the guidelines for a diabetic meal plan. Diabetics who may be using this book for blood glucose control will find that many of the dessert recipes contain some sugar. While most people with diabetes can tolerate some sugar when it is contained within a mixed meal, if you are on insulin or are prone to unstable blood glucose, please check with your physician, diabetes educator, or dietitian before using these dessert recipes.

Bread/Starch List

Each serving has 80 calories
15 grams of carbohydrate
3 grams of protein
0 grams of fat

Sliced bread	1 slice
Hot dog or hamburger bun or English muffin	1/2
Dinner roll	1 small
Tortilla, 6-inch diameter	1
Graham crackers	3 squares
Soda crackers	6
Wheat crackers	3
Rye Crisp® crackers	4
Animal crackers	8
Pretzels	3/4 oz.
Oyster crackers	24
Popcorn, air popped	3 cups
Angel food cake	1/12 cake
Frozen yogurt	1/3 cup
Sherbet	1/4 cup
Gingersnap cookies	3
Bran cereals	1/3 cup
Cooked cereals or shredded wheat	1/2 cup
Dry flaked cereals	3/4 cup
Puffed cereal	1 1/2 cup
Noodles, cooked	1/2 cup
Rice, cooked	1/3 cup
Legumes (dried peas and beans) cooked	1/3 cup
Baked beans	1/4 cup
Potatoes, mashed (with no milk or margarine added)	1/2 cup
Potatoes, baked	1 small
Sweet potato	1/3 cup
Corn	1/2 cup
Corn on the cob, 6 inches long	1
Peas or lima beans	1/2 cup
Squash, acorn or butternut	3/4 cup

Meats

Weigh meat after cooking!
Each serving has 55 calories
0 grams of carbohydrate
7 grams of protein
3 grams of fat

Lean cuts of USDA Good or Choice beef including: sirloin, chuck, round, rib-eye, brisket tenderloin, chipped beef, lean ground beef	1 oz.
Lean pork including fresh, boiled, canned or cured ham, tenderloin, center chops, leg roast	1 oz.
Veal chops and steaks	1 oz.
Chicken, turkey, or Cornish hen (no skin)	1 oz.
Fresh and frozen fish	1 oz.
Crab, lobster, scallops, shrimp, and clams	2 oz.
Tuna canned in water	1/4 cup
Pheasant, duck, and goose without skin	1 oz.
Venison, rabbit, squirrel	1 oz.
Low-fat cottage cheese	1/4 cup
Parmesan cheese	1 TB.
Cheese with 2 or less grams of fat per ounce	1 oz.
95% fat-free luncheon meat	1 oz.
Egg whites	3
Whole egg	1
Egg Substitute	1/4 cup

Combination foods are found on page 28.

Vegetables

Each serving has 25 calories
5 grams of carbohydrate
2 grams protein
0 grams fat

Choose 1/2 cup cooked or 1 cup raw servings from these:

Artichokes
Asparagus
Green and wax beans
Bean sprouts
Broccoli
Brussels sprouts
Cabbage, cooked
Carrots
Cauliflower
Eggplant
Greens
Kohlrabi
Leeks
Mushrooms, cooked
Okra
Onions, cooked
Pea pods
Peppers, cooked
Sauerkraut
Spinach, cooked
Summer squash
Tomatoes or tomato juice
Turnips
Water chestnuts
Zucchini, cooked

Fruits

Each serving has 60 calories
15 grams carbohydrate
0 grams protein
0 grams fat

Medium-sized fresh fruits including apple, orange, peach, pear, nectarine, and kiwi	1
Canned fruits in their own juice including pineapple, pears, peaches, cherries, apricots, and fruit cocktail	1/2 cup
Banana	1/2 large
Blueberries and blackberries	3/4 cup
Strawberries	1 1/4 cup
Plums	2
Cantaloupe	1/3
Grapefruit	1/2
Grapes	15
Cherries	12
Mandarin oranges	3/4 cup
Watermelon	1 1/4 cup
Dried fruit	1/4 cup
Fruit juice including apple, grapefruit, orange, pineapple	1/2 cup
Prune, cranberry, or grape juice	1/3 cup

Milk

Each serving has 90 calories
12 grams carbohydrate
8 grams protein
less than 1 gram fat

Skim, 1/2%, or 1%	1 cup
Evaporated skim milk	1/2 cup
Low-fat buttermilk	1 cup
Dry nonfat milk powder	1/3 cup
Plain nonfat milk	1 cup

Combination foods such as whole milk are found on page 28.

Fats

Each serving has 45 calories and 5 grams of fat

Unsaturated fats including	
Margarine	1 tsp.
Diet margarine	1 TB.
Mayonnaise	1 tsp.
Reduced-calorie mayonnaise	1 TB.
Nuts and seeds	1 TB.
Vegetable oil	1 tsp.
Salad dressing, mayonnaise-type	2 tsp.
Light salad dressing, mayonnaise-type	1 TB.
Salad dressing, all other types	1 TB.
Reduced-calorie salad dressing	2 TB.
Saturated fats including:	
Butter	1 tsp.
Cream, light or sour	2 TB.
Cream cheese	1 TB.
Bacon	1 slice

Free Foods

Each item has 20 or less calories per serving

Beverages including sugar-free soft drinks, club soda, carbonated water, coffee, tea, sugar-free drink mixes, bouillon, or broth	3 cups
Cranberries or rhubarb	1/2 cup
Raw vegetables including cabbage, celery, cucumber, green onion, hot peppers, mushrooms, radishes, zucchini, lettuce, and spinach	1 cup
Sugar-free hard candy, gelatin, and gum	3 servings
Sugar-free jam	2 tsp.
Sugar-free syrup	2 TB.
Catsup	2 TB.
Condiments including horseradish, mustard, taco sauce, vinegar, soy sauce, lemon juice, Worcestershire sauce, cooking wine	3 TB.
Dill pickles	3 large

Combination Foods

Food, Serving Size	Exchange Value
Biscuit or muffin, 1 small	1 bread/starch, 1 fat
Cornbread, 2-inch square	1 bread/starch, 1 fat
Party crackers, 6	1 bread/starch, 1 fat
French fries, 10	1 bread/starch, 1 fat
Pancake, 2 4-inch round	1 bread/starch, 1 fat
Waffle, 1 4-inch square	1 bread/starch, 1 fat
Stuffing, 1/4 cup	1 bread/starch, 1 fat
Taco shells, 2	1 bread/starch, 1 fat
Regular cheeses, 1 oz.	1 meat, 1 fat
2% milk, 1 cup	1 milk, 1 fat
Plain 2% yogurt, 1 cup	1 milk, 1 fat
2% milk, 1 cup	1 milk, 1 fat
Plain 2% yogurt, 1 cup	1 milk, 1 fat
Whole milk, 1 cup	1 milk, 2 fat
Plain whole-milk yogurt, 1 cup	1 milk, 2 fat
Homemade casseroles, 1 cup	2 bread/starch, 2 meat, 1 fat
Cheese pizza, 1/4 of 15 oz.	2 bread/starch, 1 meat, 1 fat
Chunky soups, 10 oz.	1 bread/starch, 1 veg., 1 meat
Cream soups, 1 cup	1 bread/starch, 1 fat
Broth-based soups, 1 cup	1 bread/starch
Cookies, 2 small	1 bread/starch, 1 fat
Ice cream, 1/2 cup	1 bread/starch, 2 fat
Snack chips, 1 oz.	1 bread/starch, 2 fat
Vanilla wafers, 6	1 bread/starch, 1 fat

Other combination foods are listed in the sections entitled Using Carryout & Fast Foods and A Snack for Every Tastebud.

Daily Meal Plans Using Food Exchanges

1000 Calories (32 grams of fat)

Breakfast
Bread/starch	1
Fruit	1
Milk, skim	1/2
Fat	1

Lunch
Bread/starch	1
Meat	2
Vegetable	1
Fruit	1
Milk, skim	1/2
Fat	1

Dinner
Bread/starch	1
Meat	3
Vegetable	1
Fruit	1
Milk, skim	1
Fat	1

Snacks
Bread/starch	-
Meat	-
Fruit	-
Milk, skim	-

1200 Calories (33 grams of fat)

Breakfast

Bread/starch	2
Fruit	1
Milk, skim	1/2
Fat	1

Lunch

Bread/starch	1
Meat	2
Vegetable	1
Fruit	1
Milk, skim	1/2
Fat	1

Dinner

Bread/starch	1
Meat	3
Vegetable	1
Fruit	1
Milk, skim	1
Fat	1

Snacks

Bread/starch	-
Meat	-
Fruit	1
Milk, skim	-

1500 Calories (38 grams of fat)

Breakfast
Bread/starch	2
Fruit	1
Milk, skim	1/2
Fat	1

Lunch
Bread/starch	2
Meat	2
Vegetable	1
Fruit	1
Milk, skim	1/2
Fat	1

Dinner
Bread/starch	2
Meat	3
Vegetable	1
Fruit	1
Milk, skim	1
Fat	2

Snacks
Bread/starch	1
Meat	-
Fruit	1
Milk, skim	-

1800 Calories (46 grams of fat)

Breakfast

Bread/starch	2
Fruit	1
Milk, skim	1/2
Fat	1

Lunch

Bread/starch	2
Meat	3
Vegetable	1
Fruit	1
Milk, skim	1/2
Fat	2

Dinner

Bread/starch	3
Meat	3
Vegetable	1
Fruit	1
Milk, skim	1
Fat	2

Snacks

Bread/starch	1
Meat	-
Fruit	1
Milk, skim	1

2000 Calories (54 grams of fat)

Breakfast

Bread/starch	3
Fruit	2
Milk, skim	1/2
Fat	2

Lunch

Bread/starch	2
Meat	3
Vegetable	2
Fruit	1
Milk, skim	1/2
Fat	2

Dinner

Bread/starch	3
Meat	3
Vegetable	1
Fruit	1
Milk, skim	1
Fat	2

Snacks

Bread/starch	1
Meat	1
Fruit	1
Milk, skim	1

Note: Use these meal plans as a guide for distributing food exchanges throughout the day to control total fat and calories. Careful measurement of food is necessary. Exchange lists (found on the previous pages) provide great variety and balance in planning menus. All of the recipes in this cookbook are analyzed for exchange values and this is noted at the end of each recipe.

A LOW-FAT SHOPPING LIST FOR YOUR KITCHEN

★ ★ ★

I f the idea of controlling fat is new for you, it may be time to make a clean sweep in the kitchen. Throw out or give away the known troublemakers.

What are the known troublemakers? The list might be endless. Chocolate and fatty candies, jars of nuts that tempt you, ice cream you scoop from your freezer, prepared cakes or cookies or bars that you're saving for a special occasion.

If you're using a solid shortening, give it away or put it away. It probably is a saturated fat. If you have loads of frozen sausages, bacon, bratwurst, hot dogs, or bologna, give them away. If you have tuna packed in oil, rinse it well in hot water before using it.

Whipped toppings are generally high in saturated fat. Try to eliminate them from your life. Check out the boxed foods and mixes you have on hand. Many packaged side dishes, such as potatoes and rice, call for margarine in preparation. You can get by with 1/4 the amount called for.

Look at your salad dressings. Are they high in fat? If so, throw them away and buy the reduced-calorie or no-oil brands.

Look at the label on your margarine. Is it made from liquid oil?

How much cheese is in the refrigerator? Is it made from skim milk? If not, invite the neighbors over and serve cheese. It is silly to think you can have these nasty foods around and not eat them. If you're serious about a low-fat diet, plan your next shopping trip from foods on this list!

Deli Case

Lean roast beef
Ham and turkey ham
Turkey and chicken breast
Part-skim farmer's cheese
Part-skim mozzarella
Breadsticks
Submarine buns
Hard rolls
Rye, French and Italian bread
Pita and sandwich pockets
Triple bean salad
Gelatin with fruit
Cranberry-orange relish
Copper penny salad
Pickled cauliflower
Corn relish
Diet chef's salad
Diet tossed salad
Dressing with chicken meat
Baked beans
Chicken to go, with no skin
Barbecued beef
Spaghetti
Chili
Beef stew
Chop suey
Almond chicken
Cheese pizzas
Soups: Vegetable beef, bean,
    vegetable chowder and
    chicken noodle
Vegetable relish tray
Fruit tray
Deluxe meat tray

Bread and Bakery

Plain breads, rolls, buns
Croutons, Wasa bread
Angel food cake
Breadsticks and English muffins
Bagels

Meat, Fish and Poultry

Sirloin sandwich steak
Plain catfish
Minute steaks
Sirloin steaks
85% lean ground beef
Ground round
Ground chuck
Pork loin chop
Pork sirloin cutlet
Pork rump roast
Canadian bacon
95% lean ham
All chicken (remove skin)
Tyson skinless chicken
Louis Rich turkey breast
Louis Rich ground turkey
Longmont turkey ham
Whole turkey
Turkey breast
Raw shrimp
Crab legs and lobster tail
All unbreaded fish fillets
Rabbit
Beef or turkey burgers
Louis Rich turkey sausage
Louis Rich frankfurters
Land O Frost chicken
Louis Rich turkey ham
Louis Rich white chicken
Any 95% lean sliced ham

Produce

All fresh fruits
All fresh vegetables except
    avocados
Potatoes and other tubers
Dried Fruits:
    Prunes
    Bordeau Dates
    Apple chips

Salad Dressings and Condiments

Limit Serving to 1 TB:
Miracle Whip Light
Weight Watchers Salad Dressing
Hellman's Light Mayonnaise
Kraft Light Salad Dressing
Estee Packaged Dressing Mixes
Kraft Oil-Free Dressings
Henri's Less Oil Dressings
Cooking wines
Bacon bits
Vinegars
Pickles
Mustard and ketchup
Worcestershire sauce
Mrs. Dash Steak Sauce

Canned Fruits and Vegetables

Any canned fruit
All fruit juices
All canned vegetables
Pork and beans (remove fat cube)
All vegetable juices

Chinese and Mexican Foods

Soy sauce
Teriyaki sauce
Water chestnuts
Chow mein noodles
La Choy Classic Dinners
Taco sauce
Taco shells
Garbonzo beans
Taco seasoning

Canned Meats

White chunky chicken
Premium white chicken
Any tuna packed in water
Salmon
Sardines in water or tomato sauce
Herring, clams, and oysters

Pasta and Legumes

All eggless pasta
Whole-wheat eggless pasta
Dried beans, peas, lentils
Dried bean soup mix
Tomato sauce and paste
Ragu Homestyle Sauce

Packaged Dinners and Side Dishes

Rice a Roni
Suzi Wan rice dishes
Country Inn Dishes (add no fat)
Lipton Rice and Sauce
Uncle Ben's rice
Near East dishes
Barley
Minute rice
Long grain and wild rice
Franco-American Spaghetti (no meat)
Cheese pizza mixes

Frozen Foods

Plain frozen vegetables
International vegetables
Birdseye Custom Cuisine
Chow mein vegetables
Microwave vegetables
Pict Sweet Express
Pasta Accents
Healthy Choice Dinners

Le Menu Lite Style:
  Turkey Divan
  Chicken Cacciatore
  Herb Roasted Chicken
Lean Cuisine:
  Chicken Marsala
  Glazed Chicken with
    vegetables
  Turkey Breast
Weight Watchers:
  Chicken Fajitas
  London Broil
All fruit juices and drinks
Pillsbury Microwave Pancakes
Aunt Jemima Pancakes
Belgian Chef Waffles
Aunt Jemima French Toast
Kelloggs NutraGrain Waffles
Microwave Super Pretzels
Tombstone or Totino's Pizza:
  Cheese and Canadian bacon
Whole fruits
Rhodes bread dough
English muffins and bagels
Ice Milk
Frozen yogurt
Sherbet and sorbet
Kemps Juice Koolers
Crystal Light Bars
Jell-O Pops
Kemps Lite Fudge Jr's
  Sugar Free Fudgesicles
Kemp's Lite Assorted Pops

Refrigerator and Dairy Products

Fruit juices and drinks
Whole fruit products
Vegetable juices
Egg substitutes
English muffins
Bagels

Skim and 1% milk
Swiss Valley Light 1/2% milk
Light Choice sour cream
Swiss Valley light sour cream
Nonfat or 1% cottage cheese
Ricotta part-skim cheese
All 1% or nonfat yogurt
Butter Buds
All stick, tub, squeeze, or diet
  margarines made from safflower,
  sunflower, corn, partially hydro-
  genated soybean, cottonseed,
  sesame, canola, or olive oil.
The P-S ratio should be 2-to-1.
Choose these tub margarines:
  Mazola, Fleischmann's, Weight
  Watchers, Promise
Borden's Lightline cheese
Light 'n Lively Cheese
Trimline cheese product
Part-skim mozzarella cheese
Mootown Snackers String Cheese
Weight Watcher's cheeses
Light and Natural Kraft Cheese
Fresh fettucini and angel hair pasta
Corn and flour tortillas

*Staples, Seasonings, Baking and
Dessert Items*

All flours and cornmeal
All spices and salt
Seasoning mixes
Molly McButter
Mrs. Dash Crispy Coating
Pam and No-stick
Sugar and substitutes
All gelatin products
Pudding mixes (made with skim milk)
Angel food and chiffon cake
Royal Light cheesecake
Pie fillings
Canned pumpkin

Cocoa
Yeast
Jelly, jam, and honey
Maple and corn syrups
Carnation Cocoa Mix
Instant dry milk
Evaporated skim milk
All coffee and tea

Breakfast cereals and products

Carnation Instant Breakfast
Shark Bites and Fun Fruits
Fruit Wrinkles and Rollups
Nature Valley Bar
Quaker Chewy Granola Bar
Oatmeal and all oat cereals
    except Cracklin' Oat Bran
Quaker Whole Wheat
Maltex, Ralston, Maypo
    Maltomeal and grits
All types of muesli (no nuts)
All bran cereals (no nuts)
All corn and rice cereals
Grape Nuts
All wheat cereals
Puffed rice and wheat
Hungry Jack Pancake Mix (made
    with skim milk)

Cookies and Candy

Archway:
    Date Filled Oatmeal
    Gingersnap
    Oatmeal Raisin
Frookies
Keebler Playland
Vanilla Wafers
Animal Crackers
Fig Newtons
Twizler's Licorice
Perky's candy and hard candies
Spicettes and Orangettes

Crackers and Soups

Knorr and Lipton soup mixes
Mrs. Grass soup mixes
Soup starters and bouillon
Progresso broth and vegetable soups
Campbell's broth soups
All Health Valley soups
Hilton's chowder
Soda and oyster crackers
Graham crackers
Thin Bits
Wheatables
Jacobsen's toast
Wasa Extra Crisp
Ak-Mak Original Crackers
Devon Melba crackers

Snacks and Soda

Orville Redenbacher's Gourmet
    Light Popcorn
Any whole popping corn
Confetti popcorn
Pretzels
Limit to 1-oz. serving:
    Combos and Chex Snack Mix
    Doritos Light Chips
All sodas and bottled waters
Beer, wine, and spirits as
    directed by your doctor

KITCHEN GADGETS THAT CUT THE FAT

★ ★ ★

Metal or plastic strainer—to drain ground beef
No-stick skillet—to minimize need for oil
No-stick loaf and muffin pans—for baked goods
No-stick baking sheet—for baking fish
No-stick saucepan—for sauces and soups
Cutting board—for slicing vegetables and trimming meats
Grater—for grating carrots and part-skim cheeses
Microwave casserole dishes—for freeze and thaw
Salad bowl with cover—for salads that keep
Steamer—for bright tender crisp vegetables
Wire whisk—to make smooth sauces
Salad Spinner—to wash and store fresh greens
Wooden spoons—for no-stick surfaces
Pastry brush—for light coats of oil or margarine
Egg separator—to use just the whites
Mini-chopper—for chopping vegetables
Roasting pan with grate—to keep meat out of fat
Broth separator—for defatting broth
Peppermill—for fresh ground taste
Measuring cups and spoons
Spatula
Slotted spoon
Ladle
Pasta portioner
Kitchen scissors
Kitchen scale
Pastry cutter

USING CARRY-OUT AND FAST FOODS

★ ★ ★

Y ou know that feeling. You're on your way home from work or a meeting or shopping and you have nothing started for dinner. A quick stop at a fast-food restaurant is tempting. But how can you use these foods without blowing your fat allowance?

Here are some good choices from a variety of fast-food restaurants. The nutrient analyses have been done by Corrine Netzer and Marion Franz. The abbreviation N/A means nutrient data were not available.

Arby's

Junior Roast Beef
Scandinavian Vegetables in Sauce
Calories: 274
Fat: 10 gm.
Sodium: 810 mg.
Cholesterol: N/A
For exchange diets, count: 1 1/2 starch/bread, 1 1/2 medium fat
meat, 2 vegetables

Roasted Chicken Boneless Breast
Rice Pilaf
Tossed Salad with Low-Calorie Italian Dressing
Calories: 434
Fat: 10 gm.
Sodium 1391 mg.
Cholesterol: N/A
For exchange diets, count: 6 lean meat, 1 1/2 starch/bread,
1 vegetable

Burger King

Chicken Tenders
Salad with Reduced-Calorie Italian Dressing
Calories: 246
Fat: 10 gm.
Sodium: 1085 mg.
Cholesterol: N/A
For exchange diets, count: 1 starch/bread, 2 medium-fat meat,
1 vegetable

Hardees

Roast Beef Sandwich
Side Salad without Dressing
Calories: 333
Fat: 12 gm.
Sodium: 868 mg.
Cholesterol: 46 mg.
For exchange diets, count: 2 starch/bread, 2 medium-fat meat,
1 vegetable

Grilled Chicken Sandwich
Calories: 310
Fat: 9 gm.
Sodium: 890 mg.
Cholesterol: 60 mg.
For exchange diets, count: 2 starch/bread, 3 lean meat

Long John Silvers

Baked Fish Dinner with Slaw and Mixed Vegetables
Calories: 387
Fat: 19 gm.
Sodium: 1298 mg.
Cholesterol: N/A
For exchange diets, count: 1 starch/bread, 4 medium-fat meat

McDonald's

Hamburger
Side Salad with Packet of Lite Vinaigrette Dressing
Calories: 380
Fat: 14 gm.
Sodium: 885 mg.
Cholesterol: 78 mg.
For exchange diets, count: 1 1/2 medium-fat meat, 2 starch/bread,
1/2 fat, 1/2 fruit

Chicken Salad Oriental with Chow Mein Noodle Topping
Packet of Red French Reduced-Calorie Dressing
Calories: 345
Fat: 7 gm.
Sodium: 730 mg.
Cholesterol: 80 mg.
For exchange diets, count: 3 lean meat, 1/2 starch/bread, 1 fat,
1 fruit

Pizza Hut

Thin and Crispy Cheese with Choice of Vegetables
1/2 of 10-inch pizza
Calories: 450
Fat: 15 gm.
Sodium and cholesterol: N/A
For exchange diets, count: 3 1/2 starch/bread, 2 medium-fat meat,
1 fat

Thick and Chewy Cheese Pizza with Choice of Vegetables
1/2 of a 10-inch pizza
Calories: 560
Fat: 14 gm.
Sodium and cholesterol: N/A
For exchange diets, count: 5 starch/bread, 3 medium-fat meat

Taco Bell

Bean Burrito
Calories: 343
Fat: 12 gm.
Sodium: 272 mg.
Cholesterol: N/A
For exchange diets, count: 3 starch/bread, 2 fat

2 Tacos
Calories: 372
Fat: 16 gm.
Sodium 158 mg.
Cholesterol: N/A
For exchange diets, count: 2 starch/bread, 4 lean meat

2 Tostados
Calories: 358
Fat: 12 gm.
Sodium: 202 mg.
Cholesterol: N/A
For exchange diets, count: 3 starch/bread, 2 medium-fat meat

Wendy's

Baked potato
Salad from the pick-up window
Calories: 360
Fat: 8 gm.
Sodium: 600 mg.
For exchange diets, count: 3 1/2 starch/bread, 1 vegetable, 1 fat

Large Chili
Calories: 360
Fat: 12 gm.
Sodium: 1485
Cholesterol: N/A
For exchange diets, count: 2 starch/bread, 3 medium-fat meat

Wendy's Continued

Chicken Breast Fillet on a Bun
Calories: 320
Fat: 10 mg.
Sodium: 500 mg.
Cholesterol: N/A
For exchange diets, count: 2 starch/bread, 3 lean meat

FROM THE DELI

★ ★ ★

The following deli items are suggested as quick meals lower in fat than other deli selections. Nutrient analysis is provided by Dick's Supermarkets in Platteville, Wisconsin.

Food, Serving Size:	Cal.	Fat gm.	Sodium mg.	Chol mg.	Exchange values
Roast Beef, (no salt), 3 oz.	198	9	56	84	3 lean meat
Ham & Turkey Ham, 3 oz.	90	3	970	50	3 lean meat
Turkey Breast, 3 oz.	161	6	75	75	3 lean meat
Part-Skim Mozzarella, 1 oz.	80	5	150	15	1 lean meat
Breadsticks, 1 large	100	2	230	2	1 starch/ bread
Submarine Buns, 1 medium	160	2	280	0	2 starch/ bread
Hard Rolls, 1	80	1	140	0	1 starch/ bread
Plain Sliced Bread, 1	80	1	140	0	1 starch/ bread
Pita & Sandwich Pockets, 1	80	1	190	0	1 starch/ bread
Triple Bean Salad, 1/2 c.	90	1	850	0	1 vegetable, 1 lean meat
Gelatin with Fruit, 1/2 c.	80	0	35	0	1 starch/ bread
Cran-Orange Relish, 1/2 c.	100	0	35	0	1 starch/ bread
Pickled Cauliflower, 1/2 c.	8	0	415	0	1 vegetable
Corn Relish, 1/2 c.	70	1	415	0	1 starch/ bread
Diet Tossed Salad	25	0	5	0	1 vegetable
Baked Beans, 1/2 c.	130	2	569	0	1 veg., 1 1/2 starch/ bread
Barbequed Beef, 3/4 c.	198	9	84	84	3 lean meat
Spaghetti, 1 c.	290	8	700	N/A	2 lean meat 2 bread/ starch, 1veg.
Chili, 1 c.	280	11	1190	N/A	2 lean meat 2 starch/ bread, 1 veg.
Chop Suey, 1 c.	220	4	1180	N/A	2 lean meat 2 starch/ bread, 1 veg.
Cheese Pizza, 1/4 of 10 oz.	164	5	396	N/A	1 lean meat 1 starch/ bread, 1 veg.

SORTING OUT THE SALAD BAR

★ ★ ★

Don't get trapped in all that fat at the salad bar. Use this sample menu as a guide for designing a carry-out main-dish salad:

3 c. Assorted Fresh Vegetables including Lettuce, Carrots, Broccoli, Cauliflower, Celery, Pepper, Mushrooms, Onions, and Tomatoes
Top with 1/4 c. Sliced Lean Turkey
1/4 c. Shredded Mozzarella Cheese,
1 oz. Alfalfa Sprouts,
1 Scoop of Croutons
1 Scoop of Chow Mein Noodles.
Drizzle 2 TB. Reduced-Calorie Creamy Dressing over all.

Calories: 390   Fat: 16 gm.
Sodium: 1068 mg.
Cholesterol: N/A
For exchange diets, count: 2 lean meat, 1 starch/bread,
3 vegetable, 3 fat

DRESSING UP CARRY-OUT FOODS

★ ★ ★

Tease your family or guests with glamourized low-fat foods from your favorite deli.

Bean Salad
To 3 cups of drained bean salad add:

- 1 c. chopped mock crab and 1 tsp. grated lemon peel. Garnish with a twisted sliced of lemon.

- 1 c. sliced artichoke hearts packed in water. Garnish the top with a sprig of fresh parsley.

- 1 c. chopped lean ham and 1/4 tsp. garlic powder. Serve on a bed of greens garnished with carrot curls.

- 1 c. finely chopped celery.

Cabbage Salad
Choose a salad with a sugar-and-vinegar type dressing, then drain well. To 3 cups of drained salad, add:

- 1 tsp. dill weed. Garnish with sprigs of fresh dill.

- 1/2 c. chopped red bell pepper, then garnish with red and green pepper rings.

- 1 c. chopped fresh pineapple. Serve in a scooped out pineapple shell.

- 1 c. chopped fresh orange sections and 1 tsp. finely grated orange peel, then garnish with a twisted section of orange.

- 1 1/2 tsp. caraway seeds. Serve in a flat bowl lined with cabbage or spinach leaves.

Carrot Salad

To 3 cups of drained carrot salad, add:

- 1/2 c. chopped dates or raisins, then serve on a lettuce leaf.

- 1 c. seeded and chopped fresh tomatoes. Garnish with cherry tomatoes.

- 1 TB. fresh basil or 1 tsp. dried basil. Garnish with a sprinkle of Parmesan cheese.

Cucumber Salad

Choose one with a clear or vinaigrette dressing, drain and add to 3 cups of salad:

- 1 tsp. fennel. Garnish with a sprig of fresh mint.

- 1 c. chopped fresh orange. Garnish with an orange wedge.

Pasta Salad

Choose one with a clear or vinaigrette dressing, drain and add to 3 cups of salad:

- 1 c. salad shrimp, 1 TB. white wine. Garnish with coarsely grated pepper.

- 1 c. chopped lean roast beef and 1 TB. red wine. Garnish with radish roses.

A Low-Fat Snack for Every Tastebud

A low-fat diet promotes a "grazing" (or frequent feeding) style of eating. This is because the fatty component in foods takes longer to be digested than carbohydrate and protein. The traditional high-fat meal promotes a feeling of fullness. As we reduce the fat in our meals, we experience true hunger between meals. Frequent eating does not have to be a problem. You can respond to true hunger between meals with a sensible snack. A good choice of snack is one that is low in fat, yet satisfies your hunger and provides some vitamins, minerals, or protein. It is essential to keep a variety of sensible snacks on hand at home. Consider this extensive list of snacks for every taste. Some of the snacks listed contain large amounts of regular sugar (see **Sweet**) and are not indicated for diabetic persons. Other snacks are high in sodium (see **Crunchy**), and are not meant for persons with high blood pressure.

Crunchy Snacks	Cal.	Fat gm.	Sodium mg.	Chol. mg.	Exchange Diets
Apple, 1 whole	81	<1	0	1	1 fruit
Asparagus, 1 c. raw pieces	30	<1	2	0	1 vegetable
Wheat toast, 1 slice with 1 tsp. jam	80	1	140	<5	1 starch
Breadsticks, 1 oz.	86	<1	444	0	1 starch
Broccoli, 1 c. floweretes	46	<1	16	0	1 vegetable
Carrots, 1 raw	31	<1	25	0	1 vegetable
Cauliflower, 1 c. flowerets	24	<1	35	0	Free
Celery, 1 stalk	6	1	90	0	1 starch
Graham crackers, 3 squares	80	1	90	0	1 starch
Finn Crisp crackers, 4	80	0	28	N/A	1 starch
Ideal Crisp Bread, 4	68	0	158	N/A	1 starch
Kavli Norwegian Thick Crackers, 2	70	0	64	N/A	1 starch
Matzo crackers, 1 oz.	115	2	N/A	0	1 1/2 starch
Melba rounds, 5 pieces	50	1	N/A	N/A	1 starch
Oyster crackers, 24	72	1	264	N/A	1 starch
Wasa crackers, 1 piece	44	0	66	N/A	1/2 starch
Saltines, 6	72	1	252	0	1 starch
Kohlrabi, 1 c.	38	<1	28	0	1 vegetable
Green pepper, 1 c. of slices	24	<1	4	0	1 vegetable
Dill pickle, 1 large	6	0	300	0	Free
Popcorn popped in oil, 3 c.	103	4	0	0	1 starch, 1 fat
Popcorn, air-popped, 3 c.	67	0	0	0	1 starch
Popcorn, microwave light variety, 4 c.	104	4	290	0	1 starch, 1 fat
Radishes, 1 c.	14	<1	16	0	1 veg.

Chewy Snacks	Cal.	Fat gm.	Sodium mg.	Chol. mg.	Exchange Diets
Dried apple slices, 4 pieces	60	<1	21	0	1 fruit
Fruit roll-up, 1/2 oz. roll	50	<1	5	0	1 fruit
Dried apricots, 7 pieces	60	<1	3	0	1 fruit
Bagel, 2 halves toasted	150	1	320	0	2 starch
English muffin, 2 halves toasted	140	2	180	n/a	2 starch
Cheese pizza with veggies, 1/8th med. pie	164	5	309	n/a	1 starch, 1 meat, 1 fat
Raisins, 2 TB.	60	0	0	4	1 fruit
Rice cake, 1 piece	35	0	0	0	1/2 starch
Flour tortilla, 1sm. broiled with 1/2 tsp. margarine and sprinkled with chili powder	72	3	n/a	n/a	1/2 starch, 1/2 fat

Savory or Salty Snacks

	Cal.	Fat gm.	Sodium mg.	Chol. mg.	Exchange Diets
Bean dip, 1/4 c. with raw veggies	90	6	n/a	0	1 fat, 1/2 starch
Lean roast beef, 1 oz.	40	2	560	n/a	1 meat
Cheese, such as Lite Line or Weight Watchers,1 oz.	50	2	410	n/a	1 meat
Mozzarella cheese, 1 oz. part-skim	80	5	190	16	1 meat
Chicken, white meat canned, 1/4 c.	45	1	115	n/a	1 fat
Crab, 3 oz.	60	<1	270	n/a	1 meat
Taco sauce, 1/4 c. as a dip with raw veggies	15	0	440	0	free
Ham, 95% lean, 1 oz.	29	1	349	13	1 meat
Pretzels, 1 oz.	110	2	470	0	1 1/2 starch
Tuna, 1/4 c. packed in water	30	<1	155	15	1 meat
Turkey, 1 oz. white meat without skin	51	2	12	21	1 meat

Sweet Snacks

	Cal.	Fat gm.	Sodium mg.	Chol. mg.	Exchange Diets
Cinnamon bagel, 2 halves toasted	166	1	320	0	2 starch
Banana, 1 9-inch whole	105	< 1	0	1	2 fruit
Blueberries, 3/4 c. fresh	61	< 1	69	0	1 fruit
Angel food cake, 1/12 cake	140	0	130	0	2 starch
Chocolate angel food cake, 1/12 cake	140	0	300	0	2 starch
Confetti angel food cake, 1/12 cake	140	0	310	0	2 starch
Lemon custard angel food cake, 1/12 cake	140	0	210	0	2 starch

Food	Cal	Fat	Sodium		Exchange
Strawberry angel food cake, 1/12 cake	140	0	160	0	2 starch
Life Savers hard candy, 1 piece	10	0	0	0	free
Jellied candy, 1 oz.	100	0	10	0	1 1/2 fruit
Licorice, 1 oz.	100	< 1	95	0	1 1/2 fruit
Bran or corn flaked cereal, 1 oz.	90	1	150	0	1 starch
Bing cherries, 12	60	2	1	0	1 fruit
Animal crackers, 7 pieces	80	2	87	0	1 starch
Molasses cookies, 1	65	2	65	n/a	1 starch
Vanilla wafers, 6	110	4	70	n/a	1 starch, 1 fat
Chunky fruit in juice, 1/2 c.	50	0	10	0	1 fruit
Sugar-free gelatin, 1/2 c.	4	0	35	0	free
Grapes, 15	60	0	6	0	1 fruit
Cone for sherbet, 1	20	0	35	0	free
Sherbet, 1/4 c.	55	< 1	n/a	n/a	1 starch
Jelly or jam, 2 tsp.	35	0	0	0	1/2 fruit
Kiwi fruit, 1 lg.	55	< 1	4	0	1 fruit
Melon, 1 cup chunks or balls	55	< 1	53	0	1 fruit
Nectarine, 1 fresh	67	< 1	0	0	1 fruit
Orange, 1 fresh	65	< 1	0	0	1 fruit
Peach, 1 large fresh	60	< 1	0	0	1 fruit
Pear, 1 fresh	60	< 1	1	0	1 fruit
Pineapple, 3/4 c. fresh or 1/2 c. canned in juice	60	< 1	1	0	1 fruit
Sugar-free pudding, 1/2 c.	70	0	65	n/a	1 starch
Plums, 2 fresh	60	0	0	0	1 fruit
Raspberries, 1 c. fresh	60	0	0	0	1 fruit
Strawberries, 1 1/4 c. fresh	60	0	1	0	1 fruit

Chocolate Snacks

Food	Cal	Fat	Sodium		Exchange
Cocoa Krispies cereal, 1 oz. dry	110	0	190	101	1 starch
Chocolate nonfat milk, 1 c.	140	< 1	155	5	1 fruit, 1 skim milk
Alba Fit and Frosty, 1 serving	76	< 1	206	0	1 skim milk
Chocolate Malt Flavor Carnation Instant Breakfast made with 1 c. skim milk	215	2	285	5	2 fruit, 2 skim milk
Chocolate pudding pop, 1	80	2	80	1	1 starch

Frozen or Creamy Snacks	Cal.	Fat gm.	Sodium mg.	Chol. mg.	Exchange Diets
Fruit and Creme Bar, 1 serving	90	1	20	n/a	1 1/2 fruit
Sorbet, 1/4 c.	60	1	6	0	1 starch
Lemon frozen fruit bar (such as Shamitoffs), 1	50	< 1	1	0	1 fruit
Fruit and juice bar (such as Dole), 1	70	< 1	6	0	1 fruit
Popsicle, 1	60	< 1	0	0	1 fruit
Ice milk, 1/2 c.	110	3	n/a	n/a	1 fat, 1 starch
Sherbet, 1/4 c.	60	<1	6	n/a	1 starch
Yogurt, frozen, 1/3 c.	70	<1	34	n/a	1 starch
Applesauce, unsweetened with cinnamon, 1/2 c.	53	0	0	2	1 fruit
Cottage cheese, 1% fat, 1/4 c.	45	1	185	4	1 meat
Yogurt, nonfat with fruit and Nutrasweet, 1 c.	100	< 1	120	na	1 skim milk

Thirst Quenching Snacks

	Cal.	Fat gm.	Sodium mg.	Chol. mg.	Exchange Diets
Low-calorie cranberry juice, 1/2 c.	24	0	4	0	free
Grape juice, 1/3 c. mixed with 1 c. sugar-free 7 Up	60	0	0	0	1 fruit
Apple cider, 1/2 c.	60	0	0	0	1 fruit
Light beer, 1 can	96	0	7	0	1 starch
Grapefruit juice, 1/2 c.	60	0	2	0	1 fruit
Sugar-free lemonade, 1 c.	4	0	0	0	free
Skim milk, 1 c.	86	< 1	126	0	1 skim milk
Orange or pineapple juice, 1/2 c.	60	0	0	0	1 fruit
Sugar-free soft drinks, 1 can	2-12	0	6-95	0	free
V-8 juice, 6 oz.	35	0	345	0	1 vegetable

Warm Snacks

	Cal.	Fat gm.	Sodium mg.	Chol. mg.	Exchange Diets
Vegetable bouillon, 1 packet Herb Ox Low Sodium	11	< 1	10	0	free
Oatmeal, 1/2 c. no salt added	69	1	1	0	1 starch
Coffee or decaffeinated coffee, 1 c.	5	0	1	0	free
Tea or herb tea	2	0	0	0	free
Vegetable beef soup, 1 c.	150	2	1140	n/a	1 starch, 1 vegetable
Chicken noodle soup, 1 c.	120	4	980	n/a	1 starch, 1 fat
Hot tomato juice, 6 oz.	30	0	550	0	1 vegetable

MENUS IN A PINCH
★ ★ ★

I f the kitchen is not your favorite place for leisure, here are some quick menus for everyday use that require common ingredients from *A Low Fat Shopping List* (see pages 34-38). When you get home late and have nothing planned for dinner, turn to this section. You'll feel in control again.

A basic menu can be created around an entree, one accompaniment, and a dessert. Add milk and bread and it's a banquet. Impulse eating doesn't have to be high fat, as you'll see from the following idea lists.

ENTREE IDEAS IN A PINCH

★ ★ ★

All measurements are for approximately 4 servings. *Menus in a Pinch* are ideas for quick low-fat meals and all measurements are approximate. Use your own discretion when adding seasonings. Work with your own kitchen inventory to make substitutions for vegetable or meat ingredients in this section.

Using pasta
The beauty of pasta is that you can start it cooking and 8 minutes later, it's just right. Use those 8 minutes to fix the rest of the meal. For perfect pasta, bring 2 quarts of water in a one-gallon pot to a boil. Do not use a small pan because it will boil over and you'll be cleaning up a messy stove. Add 8 ounces of pasta and boil rapidly (keep the bubbles coming to ensure tender noodles). Boil for 8 to 12 minutes or follow package directions. Set the timer so it doesn't overcook. Drain noodles in a colander and rinse with cold water, tossing as you rinse.

Mozzarella Macaroni
8 oz. dry macaroni, cooked and tossed with
8 ounces no added salt tomato sauce
2 tsp. dried basil
8 ounces shredded part-skim mozzarella cheese

Calories per 1/4th recipe: 337
Fat: 6 gm. Cholesterol: 15 mg.
Sodium: 163 mg.
For exchange diets, count: 3 starch/bread, 2 vegetables,
1 lean meat

Crab Spaghetti

8 oz. dry spaghetti, cooked and tossed with
8 oz. mock crab, flaked
5 oz. (or one-half of a small can) Campbell's Special Request®
  Cream of Mushroom Soup
2 tsp. dried cilantro and/or 1 TB. green chilis

Calories per 1/4 recipe: 322
Fat: 4 gm. Cholesterol: 12 mg.
Sodium: 652 mg.
For exchange diets, count: 3 starch/bread, 1 vegetable,
2 lean meat

Asparagus Fettucini

8 oz. dry fettucini, cooked and tossed with
1 lb. steamed asparagus cuts
4 oz. Parmesan cheese

Calories per 1/4 recipe: 368
Fat: 8 gm. Cholesterol: 19 mg.
Sodium: 457 mg.
For exchange diets, count: 2 vegetable, 2 lean meat,
2 1/2 starch/bread

Tuna or Chicken Linguini

8 oz. dry linguini, cooked and tossed with
8 oz. drained water-pack tuna or chicken
1 c. steamed green peas
5 oz. Campbell's Special Request® Cream of Mushroom Soup

Calories per 1/4 recipe: 356
Fat: 4 gm. Cholesterol: 18 mg.
Sodium: 351 mg.
For exchange diets, count: 3 starch/bread, 1 lean meat,
2 vegetable

Using flour tortillas

Flour tortillas are made for stuffing. For quickest results, stuff them, rolling seam side down and place in a pan that has been sprayed with nonstick cooking spray. Put them in the microwave for 2 1/2 to 4 minutes. Conventional baking at 375° F. for 20 minutes also works. Always serve chopped lettuce and/ or tomatoes on the side. For a topping, try blenderized part-skim ricotta or nonfat cottage cheese.

Ham and Vegetable Tortilla

Stuff 8 6-in. flour tortillas with a mixture of:
8 oz. slivered lean ham
2 oz. shredded part-skim cheese of choice
2 c. steamed vegetables of choice

Calories per 1/4 recipe: 323
Fat: 15 gm. Cholesterol: 35 mg.
Sodium: 430 mg.
For exchange diets, count: 2 starch/bread, 1 fat,
2 lean meat

Chicken and Chili Tortilla

Stuff 8 6-in. flour tortillas with a mixture of:
8 oz. cooked chicken pieces
5 oz. Campbell's Special Request® Cream of Chicken Soup
2 TB. green chilis

Calories per 1/4 recipe: 257
Fat: 6 gm. Cholesterol: 41 mg.
Sodium: 497 mg.
For exchange diets, count: 2 starch/bread,
2 lean meat

Tortillas with Leftovers

Stuff 8 6-in. flour tortillas with a mixture of:

8 oz. any leftover meat such as sirloin
1/4 c. chopped onion
1/4 c. chopped green pepper
8 oz. no added salt tomato sauce
2 tsp. taco seasoning

Calories per 1/4 recipe: 250
Fat: 4 gm. Cholesterol: 40 mg.
Sodium: 356 mg.
For exchange diets, count: 1 vegetable, 2 starch/bread,
1 lean meat

Kidney Bean Tortilla

Stuff 8 6-in. flour tortillas with a mixture of:

16 oz. (1 small can) drained kidney beans
1/2 c. chopped scallions
2 TB. green chilis
4 oz. shredded part-skim cheese

Calories per 1/4 recipe: 327
Fat: 7 gm. Cholesterol: 15 mg.
Sodium: 866 mg.
For exchange diets, count: 2 starch/bread, 2 vegetable,
2 lean meat

Using vegetables

Chicken-Topped Potatoes
Bake 4 potatoes. Lay the potato on its flat side and slice across it both ways, creating a middle cavity. Stuff with a mixture of:
8 oz. cooked chicken pieces
5 oz. Campbell's Special Request® Cream of Celery soup
2 TB. green chilis or scallions
Cover and microwave for 3 minutes on high power.

Calories per 1/4 recipe: 338
Fat: 4 gm. Cholesterol: 44 mg.
Sodium: 234 mg.
For exchange diets, count: 3 starch/bread, 2 lean meat

Snappy Stuffed Peppers
Clean 4 peppers and remove seeds. Mix the following together and stuff the peppers:
1 c. quick rice
1/2 c. water
8 oz. no added salt tomato sauce
8 oz. shredded mozzarella cheese
2 tsp. basil
Cover stuffed peppers and microwave for 15 minutes on 50% power.

Calories per 1/4 recipe: 300
Fat: 10 gm. Cholesterol: 30 mg.
Sodium: 629 mg.
For exchange diets, count: 2 lean meat, 2 starch/bread,
1 vegetable

Leftover Vegetable Stir-Fry
Combine the following in a no-stick skillet:
4 c. leftover steamed vegetables
2 c. drained canned chicken or salmon
2 tsp. dill weed
1 TB. vegetable oil
Stir-fry until heated through.

Calories per 1/4 recipe: 130
Fat: 5 gm. Cholesterol: 44 mg.
Sodium: 39 mg.
For exchange diets, count: 1 vegetable, 2 lean meat

Broiled Asparagus Main Dish
1 lb. asparagus, cleaned, stemmed, and steamed until tender
Place on broiler-proof pan and top with:
8 oz. shredded part-skim farmer cheese
1 c. croutons
Broil for 5 minutes or until cheese bubbles.

Calories per 1/4 recipe: 238
Fat: 10 gm. Cholesterol: 30 mg.
Sodium: 417 mg.
For exchange diets, count: 3 vegetable, 2 lean meat, 1 fat

Using Meats
When you have a main meat and need something quick to dress
it up, try the following:

Ham Steak Marinade
Mix 1/4 cup each of Worcestershire sauce, brown sugar, and
lemon juice. Marinate 1 lb. lean ham steak for 20 minutes, then
broil.

Calories per 1/4 recipe: 191
Fat: 4 gm. Cholesterol: 74 mg.
Sodium: 1388 mg.
For exchange diets, count: 3 lean meat, 1/2 starch/bread

Round Steak in Beer

Mix 1/2 tsp. garlic powder, 1 tsp. sugar, and 1 can beer. Marinate 1 lb. lean trimmed round steak 20 minutes, then broil.

Calories per 1/4 recipe: 192
Fat: 4 gm. Cholesterol: 72 mg.
Sodium: 56 mg.
For exchange diets, count: 3 lean meat, 1/2 starch/bread

Teriyaki White Fish

Marinate 1 lb. white fish fillets in 1/2 c. teriyaki sauce for 20 minutes, then broil.

Calories per 1/4 recipe: 119
Fat: 1 gm. Cholesterol: 47 mg.
Sodium: 1446 mg.
For exchange diets, count: 2 lean meat

Italian Grilled Chicken

Marinate 1 lb. skinless chicken pieces in 1/2 c. reduced-calorie Italian dressing for 20 minutes, then broil.

Calories per 1/4 recipe: 169
Fat: 6 gm. Cholesterol: 69 mg.
Sodium: 297 mg.
For exchange diets, count: 3 lean meat

Italian Steamed Chicken

Place skinned pieces of 3 lb. chicken in microwave casserole dish. Mix 8 oz. no added salt tomato sauce with 1/2 tsp. garlic powder and 1 tsp. each of oregano, basil, sugar, and lemon juice. Pour sauce over chicken and cover. Microwave at 70% power for 15 to 18 minutes.

Calories per 1/4 recipe: 163
Fat: 4 gm. Cholesterol: 67 mg.
Sodium: 73 mg.
For exchange diets, count: 3 lean meat

Chili Meatloaf

Mix 1 lb. lean ground turkey, pork, or beef with 1 TB. chili powder. Place in microwave-proof pan and microwave for 8 to 10 minutes on high power. Drain well.

Calories per 1/4 recipe (using ground turkey): 129
Fat: 2 gm. Cholesterol: 67 mg.
Sodium: 71 mg.
For exchange diets, count: 3 lean meat

Chicken or Fish Fillets

Pat 1 lb. of skinless, boneless chicken pieces or fish fillets dry. Roll in skim milk and baking mix, such as Bisquick. Place on baking sheet and dot each piece with 1/2 tsp. margarine. Season with lemon pepper or garlic powder or paprika. Bake fish for 20 to 25 minutes and chicken for 40 to 45 minutes at 400° F.

Calories per 1/4 recipe: 191
Fat: 5 gm. Cholesterol: 67 mg.
Sodium: 232 mg.
For exchange diets, count: 3 lean meat, 1/2 starch/bread

Accompaniments in a Pinch

After the entree is started, brouse through this list of accompaniments to quickly complete the main meal. All measurements are for four servings.

Coleslaw in a Jiffy

Mix 2 c. shredded cabbage with 1/2 c. reduced-calorie coleslaw dressing.

Calories per 1/4 recipe: 53
Fat: 2 gm. Cholesterol: 2 mg.
Sodium: 260 mg.
For exchange diets, count: 2 vegetable

Pea Salad
Mix 1 c. each of thawed green peas, tomatoes, and celery with
1/2 c. reduced-calorie 1000 Island dressing.

Calories per 1/4 recipe: 89
Fat: 1 gm. Cholesterol: 2 mg.
Sodium: 322 mg.
For exchange diets, count: 1 starch/bread

Old-Fashioned Cukes
Slice 2 cucumbers and 1 onion into a shallow bowl and cover with
1 tsp. salt and 1 tray of ice cubes. Allow to sit for 30 minutes.
Meanwhile mix 1/4 c. sugar and 1/2 c. vinegar. Drain vegetables
and combine in a bowl with dressing. This will keep in the
refrigerator for 3 days.

Calories per 1/4 recipe: 72
Fat: 0 Cholesterol: 0
Sodium: 0
For exchange diets, count: 1 fruit, 1 vegetable

Tomato Medley
Slice 1 tomato, 1 cucumber, and 1 green pepper into a salad bowl.
Pour 1/2 c. reduced-calorie creamy Italian dressing over the top.

Calories per 1/4 recipe: 59
Fat: 3 gm. Cholesterol: 2 mg.
Sodium: 243 mg.
For exchange diets, count: 1 vegetable, 1/2 fat

Sugar and Sprouts
Steam 2 c. Brussels sprouts, then dot with 2 tsp. lemon juice and
2 TB. brown sugar.

Calories per 1/4 recipe: 50
Fat: 0 Cholesterol: 0
Sodium: 0
For exchange diets, count: 2 vegetable

Stuffed Squash

Combine 1/2 c. raisins or finely chopped apples with 2 TB. brown sugar. Stuff into 2 halves of an acorn squash. Place in a casserole dish, cover, and microwave for 12 to 15 minutes on high power.

Calories per 1/4 recipe: 127
Fat: less than 1 gm. Cholesterol: 0
Sodium: 5 mg.
For exchange diets, count: 2 starch/bread

Low-Fat Stuffing on the Stove

The commercial stuffing mixes are high in sodium that can't be removed, but you can control the fat content. Add just 1/4 of the margarine called for in package directions. In most cases this will be just 1 TB. instead of 1/4 c. Substitute chicken broth for the remaining fat.

Calories per 1/2-c. serving : 117
Fat: 2 gm. Cholesterol: n/a
Sodium: 580 mg.
For exchange diets, count: 1 starch/bread, 1 vegetable, 1/2 fat

DESSERTS IN A PINCH
★ ★ ★

If you're the type that likes a sweet at the end of the meal, this list will quickly delight you.

Fruits in Syrup
Mix 2 c. fresh, canned, or frozen fruit with 2 TB. lemon juice and 2 TB. grenadine.

Calories per 1/4 recipe: 80
Fat: 0 Cholesterol: 0
Sodium: 0
For exchange diets, count: 1 1/2 fruit

Fruits in Wine
Mix 2 c. fresh, canned, or frozen fruit with 2 TB. white wine and 2 TB. sugar.

Calories per 1/4 recipe: 80
Fat: 0 Cholesterol: 0
Sodium: 0
For exchange diets, count: 1 1/2 fruit

Iced Coffee
Pour your favorite coffee into a mug and top with 1/4 c. ice milk.

Calories per serving: 46
Fat: 1 gm. Cholesterol: 4 mg.
Sodium: 26 mg.
For exchange diets, count: 1/2 starch/bread

Fruit and Cream

Heat 1 c. applesauce, pineapple sauce, or cranberry relish for 3 minutes on high power in the microwave. Use as a topping for 2 c. of ice milk or frozen yogurt.

Calories per 1/4 recipe: 140
Fat: 3 gm. Cholesterol: 9 mg.
Sodium: 54 mg.
For exchange diets, count: 2 fruit, 1/2 fat

Apples in Maple Syrup

Peel and core 4 apples suited to baking (Winesaps, Jonathans, or McIntosh varieties are best). Place apples in a baking dish, then drizzle with 1/2 c. maple syrup. Cover and microwave for 6 to 9 minutes on high power.

Calories per 1/4 recipe: 110
Fat: less than 1 gm. Cholesterol: 0
Sodium: 8 gm.
For exchange diets, count: 2 fruit

SPRING & SUMMER

MENUS & RECIPES

A Month of Low-Fat Dinner Menus for Spring and Summer

These dinner menus feature common foods and selected recipes from this book (noted with*). Use the dinner menus together with breakfast and lunch menus on page 70 to create a 40-gm. fat (or 1500-calorie) diet plan.

WEEK ONE	WEEK TWO	WEEK THREE	WEEK FOUR
1 serving *White Fish Creole 1/2 c. Quick Rice 1 c. Fresh Greens with 2 TB. No Oil Dressing 1 serv. *Mile High Peach Pie 1 c. Skim Milk	1 serv. *Meat Loaves Italiano 1/2 c. Steamed Potatoes 1 serv. *Lemon Zucchini 1 sl. Angelfood Cake with 1 c. Fresh Strawberries 1 c. Skim Milk	1 serv. *Spring Turkey Salad 1 Toasted Onion Bagel with 1 tsp. Margarine 1 serv. *Blueberry and Pineapple Dessert 1 c. Skim Milk	1 Serv. *Tortilla Cheeseburgers 1 c. Fresh Greens with 1 serv. *Tomato Dressing 1/2 c. Sliced Oranges 1 c. Skim Milk
1 serving *Layered Summer Salad 2 lg. Breadsticks 1/4 Cantelope Marinated in Gingerale 1 c. Skim Milk	1/3 c. Grape Juice 1 serv. *Easy Seafood Salad 1 serv. *Onion Cheese Supper Bread 1/2 c. Sugar-Free Vanilla Pudding with Raisins 1 c. Skim Milk	1 serv. *Bean Casserole Ole' 1 serv. *Cornbread with Chilis 1 c. Tomato Slices 1/2 c. Cranberry Juice 1 c. Skim Milk	1 serv. *Mediterranean Supper 1 sl. White Bread from Frozen Dough with 1 tsp. Margarine 1/2 c. Applesauce over 1/2 c. Ice Milk 1 c. Skim Milk
1 serv. *Sirloin Barbeque 1/2 c. Steamed Carrots 1 serv. *Spaghetti Salad 15 Fresh Green Grapes 1 c. Skim Milk	1 serv. *Cornflake Chicken 1/2 c. Mashed Potatoes with 1 tsp. Margarine 1 serv. *Eggplant & Tomato Parmesan 12. Bing Cherries 1 c. Skim Milk	3 oz. Lean Broiled Hamburger on a Wheat Bun 1 serv. *Carrot Marinade 1 c. Sliced Watermelon 1 c. Skim Milk	1 serv. *Seafood & Summer Vegetables 1 sl. Broiled Garlic Toast 1 serv. *Peach Ambrosia 1 c. Skim Milk
1 serv. *Garden Pizza 1 serv. *Old Fashioned Cucumbers 1/2 Frozen Banana 1 c. Skim Milk	1/2 c. Chilled No Added Salt Tomato Juice 1 serv. *Broccoli & Cheese Enchiladas 4 Carrot Sticks 15 Red Grapes 1 c. Skim Milk	1 serv. *Filling Spinach Salad 1 *Apricot Muffin 1/2 c. Blueberries with 1 c. Nonfat Vanilla Yogurt on top	1 serv. *Mexican Turkey Salad 1 Broiled Flour Tortilla with 1 tsp. Margarine 1 serv. *Honeydew Whip 1 c. Skim Milk
1 serv. *Mediterannean Cod Baked Potato with Margarine 1 c. Fresh Greens with 1 serv.*Lemon & Basil Dressing 1/2 c. Sorbet 1 c. Skim Milk	1 serv. *Pizza Salad 1 Kaiser Roll with 1/2 tsp. Margarine 1 Granny Smith Apple 1 c. Skim Milk	1 serv. *Chicken Divan 1 sl. Rye Bread with Margarine 1 serv. *Summer Vegetable Mold 1 Nectarine 1 c. Skim Milk	3 oz. Sauteed Chicken Breast 1 Baked Potato 1 serv. *Escalloped Cabbage 1 Fresh Pear 1 c. Skim Milk
1 serv.*Baked Burrito 1 serv. *Tex Mex Slaw 1/2 c.Fresh Pineapple Slices 1 c. Skim Milk	1 serv. *Shrimp Casserole 1 serv. *Cucumber and Leek Salad 1 sl. Wheat Toast 1/2 c. Orange Slices marinated in Wine Cooler 1 c. Skim Milk	1 serv. *Pork and Black Bean Stir-Fry 4 Radishes 1 serv. *Honey of a Waldorf Salad 6 Vanilla Wafers 1 c. Skim Milk	1 serv. *Hot Crab with Vegetables 1 Wheat Roll with 1 tsp. Margarine 1/2 c. Fresh Pineapple over 1/2 c. Lime Sherbet 1 c. Skim Milk
1 serv. *Turkey Rollups over Tender Cooked Fettucine 4 Cherry Tomatoes 1/2 c. Frozen Yogurt 1 c. Skim Milk	1 serv. *Grilled Pork Kabobs 1 sl. French Bread 1 serv. *10-Calorie Molded Salad 1 serv. *Peach Melba Meringue Pie 1 c. Skim Milk	1 serv. *Bayou Fish Stew with 1 sl. Sourdough Bread 1 c. Fresh Veggies with 1 TB. Red.-Cal. Dressing 1/2 c. Raspberry Sherbet 1 c. Skim Milk	1 serv. *Zucchini Lasagne 1 c. Fresh Greens with 1 TB. Reduced-Calorie Italian Dressing 1 serv. *Frozen Grasshopper Dessert 1 c. Skim Milk

A Week of Breakfast and Lunch Menus for Spring and Summer

	Breakfast	Lunch	Snacks
Monday	1/2 c. Oatmeal with 2 TB. Raisins 1 sl.Wheat Toast & 1 tsp. Margarine 1/2 c. Skim Milk	1 oz. Farmers Cheese & 1 oz. Lean Turkey on 2 sl. Rye Bread with 1 tsp. Margarine & Mustard 1/2 c. Tomato Juice 1 Large Apple 1/2 c. Skim Milk	1 oz. Pretzels 1 Oranges
Tuesday	1 Whole Bagel Toasted with 2 tsp. Peanut Butter 1/2 c. Grapefruit Juice 1/2 c. Skim Milk	1 Large Baked Potato topped with 1/2 c. Browned Ground Beef and 1/4 c. Tomato Sauce and 1/4 Cantelope 1/2 c. Vanilla Yogurt on top	4 sq. Graham Crackers 1/2 c. Apple Juice
Wednesday	3/4 c. Flaked Cereal with 1/2 Banana 1 sl. French Bread toasted with 1 tsp. Margarine 1/2 c. Skim Milk	1/2 c. Tuna with 1 c. Fresh chopped Vegetables and 1 TB. No Oil Dressing 8 Wheat Crackers 1 Granny Smith Apple 1/2 c. Skim Milk	5 Melba Rounds 1/2 c. Pineapple Juice
Thursday	1 English Muffin Toasted with 2 Tsp. Margarine 1/2 c. Orange Juice 1/2 c. Skim Milk	2 sm. Soft Shell Tacos with 2 oz. Seasoned Ground Turkey 1 c. Chopped Lettuce & Tomato 1 Fresh Pear 1/2 c. Skim Milk	3 c. Air Popcorn 1 Apple
Friday	1/2 c. Bran Cereal 1 sl. Raisin Toast with 1 tsp. Margarine 1/2 c. Pineapple Chunks 1/2 c. Skim Milk	2 oz. GrilledBreast of Chicken on a Bun with Mustard 1 c. Steamaed Green Beans with 1 tsp. Margarine 12 Grapes 1/2 c. Skim Milk	7 Animal Crackers 2 Plums
Saturday	1/2 c. Maltomeal 1 Bran Muffin 1/2 Pineapple Juice 1/2 c. Skim Milk	1 c. Tomato Soup 4 Wheat Crackers 1/2 c. Low Fat Cottage Cheese 1/2 c. Mixed Fruit 1/2 c. Skim Milk	1/4 c. Sherbet with 1 Kiwi fruit
Sunday	2 sm. Pancake with 1/2 c. Applesauce and Cinnamon on top 1/2 c. Skim Milk	2 oz. Lean Ham 2 lg. Breadsticks Radishes, Carrots & Celery 1 c. Watermelon Chunks 1/2 c. Skim Milk	1/2 c. Blueberries & 1 Molasses Cookie

Use these breakfast and lunch menus together with dinner menu suggestions on page ** to create a 40-gm. fat (or 1500-calorie) diet plan.

SPECIAL OCCASION MENUS
FOR SPRING AND SUMMER

Confirmation or First Communion Dinner
*Hawaiian Pork
Baked Potatoes
Fresh Vegetables with
*Creamy Cucumber Dressing
Wheat Dinner Rolls with Margarine
*Strawberry Alaska

Easter Sunday
*Gourmet Chicken with Cheese
Steamed Broccoli
*Glazed Lemon Muffins
*Easter Salad
*Spring Parfait

Memorial Day
*Grilled Pork A La Orange
*Green Bean and Dilly Stir-fry
*Wild Rice Salad
*Rhubarb Crunch

Ladies' Luncheon
*Fresh Mushroom Soup with Rye Crisp Crackers
*Chicken Chestnut Salad
*Fancy Marinated Tomatoes
*Tortoni Cafetta

*Recipe included. Check index for page number.

Graduation Buffet
*Blue Cheese Dip for Veggies
*Cocktail Crab Dip with Wheat Crackers
*Love My Cheddar Cheese Ball with Breadsticks
*Curried Chicken Salad
*Lasagna Salad
*Wild Rice and Vegetable Salad
*Pineapple in Poppyseed Dressing
*Cheesecake with Rhubarb Sauce

Golf Outing
*Spicy Guacamole with Tortilla Crisps
*Lemon Chicken for Company
*Antipasto Salad
*Summer Vegetable Medley
*Stand Up for Strawberry Pie

Fourth of July
*Western Broil
*Fabulous French Bread
*Party Potato Salad
*Lean Bean Salad
*Oatbran Crunchies

Family Reunion
*Roast Pork Loin with Cumberland Sauce
*Italian Potato Salad
*Summer Baked Beans
*Lemon Strawberry Supreme

*Recipe included. Check index for page number.

Summer Brunch

Cranraspberry Cocktail with Gingerale
*Eggs for a Bunch
*Asparagus Chef Salad
*Cold Vegetable Pasta with Lemon
*Summer Herb Buttermilk Bread
*Oatbran Blueberry Muffins
*Frozen Chocolate Cheatcake

Kid's Birthday Party

*Party Popcorn
*Deep Dish Pizza
*Want More Salad
*Zucchini Brownies
*Moonbeam Punch

Labor Day Cookout

*Cajun Fish on the Grill
*Sinless Scalloped Corn
*Cucumbers with Honey Dressing
*Oat and Zucchini Bread
*Peaches and Cheese Pie

For Casual Summer Evening Entertaining

*My Favorite Gazpacho
*Fancy Red Snapper
*Stuffed Tomato Salad
*Marinated Mushrooms
*Strawberries 'n Creme

*Recipe included. Check index for page number.

BLUE CHEESE DIP FOR VEGGIES
YIELD: 1/2 c. OR 4 2-TB. SERVINGS

★ ★ ★

> 1/3 c. low-fat cottage cheese
> 1 oz. blue cheese
> 2 TB. nonfat yogurt
> 1 1/2 tsp. minced scallion

Place all ingredients in a blender; blend until smooth. Chill and serve with raw vegetable dippers such as carrots, celery, broccoli, radishes, cauliflower, asparagus and cherry tomatoes.

Calories per 2-TB. serving: 44
Fat: 2 gm. Cholesterol: 6 mg.
Sodium: 188 mg.
For exchange diets, count: 1 fat

Preparation time: 10 min.

COCKTAIL CRAB DIP
YIELD: 1 1/2 C. OR 6 1/4-C. SERVINGS

★ ★ ★

1/4 c. toasted almonds
4 oz. light cream cheese (look for 50% fat reduced)
2 TB. minced onion
1 tsp. horseradish
1 tsp. lemon juice
Dash of Worcestershire sauce
1/8 tsp. salt
1/8 tsp. pepper
1/4 c. skim milk
4 oz. shredded crab or mock crab

Heat oven to 375° F. Spread almonds in a flat pan and place in oven for 10 minutes. Remove when browned. Combine all other ingredients and place in a casserole dish. Place almonds on top. Bake for 20 minutes or until bubbly. Serve with low-fat wheat crackers.

Calories per 1/4-c. serving: 115
Fat: 7 gm. Cholesterol: 13 mg.
Sodium: 150 mg.
For exchange diets, count: 1 fat, 1 lean meat

Preparation time: 30 min.

FRESH MUSHROOM SOUP
YIELD: 4 1 1/2-c. SERVINGS

★ ★ ★

1 1/2 lb. fresh mushrooms
8 scallions
1/2 tsp. thyme
1/4 tsp. black pepper
1 TB. Dijon mustard
1/2 c. red wine
1 qt. fat-free no added salt
    chicken broth
1 c. plain non-fat yogurt

Chop mushrooms and scallions into bite-sized pieces. Place in non-stick Dutch oven and cook with red wine until tender. Add thyme, pepper, mustard and chicken broth. Bring to a boil and simmer for 15 minutes. Add yogurt, stirring just to blend, and serve.

Calories per 1 1/2-c. serving: 105
Fat: 0   Cholesterol: 0
Sodium: 145 mg.
For exchange diets, count: 1 bread/starch, 1 vegetable

Preparation time: 25 min.

LOVE MY CHEDDAR CHEESE BALL
YIELD: 2 C. OR 8 1/4-C. SERVINGS

★ ★ ★

1 c. non-fat cottage cheese
4 oz. light cheddar cheese (label says part-skim)
1 TB. chopped pimiento
1 1/2 tsp. minced onion
1/2 tsp. Worcestershire sauce
1/8 tsp. cayenne
2 TB. chopped fresh parsley

Blenderize cottage cheese until smooth. Grate cheddar cheese. Combine all ingredients except parsley in a medium-size bowl. Chill in the freezer for 30 minutes and then form mixture into a ball. Roll in parsley and serve on a plate with low-fat wheat crackers.

Calories per 1/4-c. serving: 55
Fat: 2 gm. Cholesterol: 9 mg.
Sodium: 244 mg. (To reduce sodium, use low-sodium cheese.)
For exchange diet, count: 1/2 fat, 1/2 skim milk

Preparation time: 50 min.

MOONBEAM PUNCH
YIELD: 1 GALLON OR 16 8-OZ. SERVINGS

★ ★ ★

1 c. water
1/4 c. fresh mint leaves
1 1/2 c. sugar
1 c. lemon juice
1 quart ice water
2 qt. gingerale
Fresh lemon wedges
1 qt. lemonade or gingerale
   for ice ring

Bring water and sugar to a boil and pour over fresh mint leaves
in a shallow bowl. Cool to room temperature and remove leaves.
Combine mint-flavored water with remaining ingredients in a
punch bowl. Use gingerale or lemonade as an ice ring. Use fresh
lemon wedges for garnish.

Calories per 8-oz. serving: 99
Fat: 0 Cholesterol: 0
Sodium: 5 mg.
For exchange diets, count: 1 1/2 fruit

Preparation time: 30 min.

MY FAVORITE GAZPACHO
YIELD: 8 3/4-C. SERVINGS

★ ★ ★

4 lg. ripe tomatoes, peeled,
   seeded and chopped

1 c. no added salt tomato juice

1 c. chopped and peeled
   cucumber

1 avocado, peeled and chopped

1 red bell pepper, chopped

2 tsp. chopped jalapeno
   pepper

1/4 c. chopped scallions

2 TB. lemon juice

1/2 tsp. garlic powder

1/4 tsp. salt (optional)

1 tsp. sugar or substitute

Combine all ingredients and marinate in the refrigerator for at
least 30 minutes. Serve as a salad or use as a dip with tortillas.
Gazpacho keeps well for 3 days in the refrigerator.

Calories per 3/4 c.-serving: 75
Fat: 4 gm.   Cholesterol: 0
Sodium: 80 mg. with salt; 19 mg. without salt
For exchange diets, count: 2 vegetable, 1 fat.

Preparation time: 50 min.

Note: To make a crunchy low-fat tortilla, spray flour tortillas
with nonstick cooking spray, sprinkle with chili powder, and bake
at 200° F. for 15 minutes. Cool before serving.

PARTY POPCORN
YIELD: 2 QUARTS OR 4 2-CUP SERVINGS

★ ★ ★

8 c. popped corn
1 TB. dill weed
2 tsp. finely grated lemon
  rind
1/4 tsp. garlic powder
1/2 tsp. pepper
2 TB. margarine, melted

Place popped corn into a 3-quart baking pan. Mix seasonings
with melted margarine. Pour over popped corn and stir. Bake at
200° F. for 1 hour, stirring every 15 minutes. Cool to room
temperature and transfer to an air-tight container. To use after
several days, simply rewarm in the oven at 200° F. for 10
minutes.

Calories per 2-cup serving: 96
Fat: 6 gm. Cholesterol: 0
Sodium: 66 mg.
For exchange diets, count: 1/2 bread/starch, 1 fat

Preparation time: 1 hr, 15 min.

SPICY GUACAMOLE WITH TORTILLA CRISPS
YIELD: 1 C. OR 8 2-TB. SERVINGS

★ ★ ★

1 avocado, seeded, peeled and
  cut up
1/2 c. nonfat yogurt
2 TB. light mayonnaise
1/4 tsp. garlic powder
1/4 tsp. salt
1/4 tsp. cayenne

Tortilla Crisps:
4 6-inch flour tortillas
Nonstick cooking spray
2 tsp. chili powder

Peel avocado, cut up, and place in a blender with other
ingredients. Blend smooth. Chill. Spray tortillas with nonstick
cooking spray (such as Pam®), and sprinkle with chili powder.
Broil for 3 minutes. Cut into triangles and serve with guacamole
dip.

Calories per 2-TB. dip and 1/2 tortilla: 110
Fat: 6 gm. Cholesterol: less than 1 mg.
Sodium: 140 mg.
For exchange diets, count: 1 fat, 1 vegetable, 1 bread/starch

Preparation time: 30 min.

Apricot Muffins
Yield: 24 muffins

* * *

2 c. flour
1/4 c. white sugar
1/2 c. brown sugar
1 TB. baking powder
3/4 tsp. salt
2 tsp. pumpkin pie spice
1/2 c. oatmeal
1 c. chopped dried apricots
1/2 c. chopped walnuts
1 egg or 1/4 c. liquid egg
    substitute
1 1/2 c. skim milk
1/3 c. vegetable oil

Preheat oven to 350° F. Combine flour, brown sugar, baking powder, salt, pumpkin pie spice, and oatmeal in a large bowl. Stir in apricots and walnuts. Use an egg beater to combine eggs, milk, and oil in a small bowl. Pour liquid into dry ingredients, stirring just to moisten. Spoon batter into muffin cups, filling two-thirds full. Bake for 25 to 30 minutes or until muffins are brown.

Calories per muffin: 119
Fat: 5 gm. Cholesterol: 14 mg. with real eggs
Sodium: 120 mg.
For exchange diets, count: 1 bread/starch, 1 fat

Preparation time: 45 min.

Note: If you do not have pumpkin pie spice on hand, substitute: 1 tsp. cinnamon, 1/2 tsp. ginger, 1/4 tsp. nutmeg, 1/8 tsp. ground cloves.

Cornbread with Chilis
Yield: 8-inch square pan or 12 squares

* * *

1 c. flour
1 c. cornmeal
2 TB. sugar
4 tsp. baking powder
1/4 tsp. salt
1 egg or 1/4 c. liquid egg
  substitute
2 TB. vegetable oil
2 TB. diced green chilis (may
  use canned or fresh)

Preheat oven to 375° F. Combine flour, cornmeal, sugar, baking powder, and salt in a large bowl. Using an egg beater, combine egg, skim milk, and oil. Pour liquid into the dry ingredients. Add chilis. Stir just until blended. Batter will be lumpy. Pour into an 8-inch square pan that has been sprayed with nonstick cooking spray. Bake for 25 minutes or until an inserted toothpick returns clean.

Calories per square: 119
Fat: 3 gm.   Cholesterol: 21 mg. with egg; 1 mg. with substitute
Sodium: 166 mg.
For exchange diets, count: 1 bread/starch, 1 fat

Preparation time: 45 min.

FABULOUS FRENCH BREAD
YIELD: 2 LOAVES OR 40 SLICES

★ ★ ★

2 pkg. dry yeast
1/2 c. water
1/2 tsp. sugar
2 TB. sugar
2 TB. margarine
2 tsp. salt
2 c. boiling water
7 1/2 c. flour
Cornmeal to dust pans

Dust 2 French bread loaf pans with cornmeal. Dissolve yeast in
1/2 c. water and stir in 1/2 tsp. sugar. Combine 2 TB. sugar,
margarine, salt, and boiling water in a large mixing bowl. Cool to
lukewarm and stir in yeast. Slowly add flour, processing with
food processor or electric mixer or by hand until dough is smooth
and elastic. Cover and allow to rise until double in bulk. Form
into 2 loaves. Place a pan of boiling water in the bottom of the
oven. Bake in preheated 400° oven for 20 minutes. Cool for 10
minutes, then remove loaves from pan and cool on a rack.

Calories per slice: 96
Fat: 1 gm. Cholesterol: 0
Sodium: 107 mg.
For exchange diets, count: 1 bread/starch

Preparation time: 90 min.

Speed Alert: This recipe takes 90 minutes when bread is
allowed to rise in warm place.

GLAZED LEMON MUFFINS
YIELD: 18 MUFFINS

★ ★ ★

2/3 c. sugar
1/3 c. vegetable oil
1 egg or 1/4 c. liquid egg
  substitute
1 c. low-fat lemon yogurt
1 TB. grated fresh lemon peel
1 tsp. soda
2 c. flour

Glaze:
1/4 c. lemon juice
2 TB. sugar

Preheat oven to 375° F. In mixing bowl, cream sugar and oil.
Beat in egg, yogurt, and lemon peel. Combine soda and flour,
then stir into batter just until all is moistened. Spoon batter into
greased or lined muffin tins. Bake for 20 minutes. To glaze: Use
a toothpick to poke 5 holes in each muffin. Combine lemon juice
and sugar in a glass measuring cup and microwave for 25 seconds
to dissolve sugar. Stir. Pour a small amount of glaze over each
muffin.

Calories per muffin: 125
Fat: 4 gm. Cholesterol: 15 mg. with real egg
Sodium: 45 mg.
For exchange diets, count: 1 bread/starch, 1 fat

Preparation time: 40 min.

Oat and Zucchini Bread
Yield: 1 loaf or 18 slices

★ ★ ★

1 sm. zucchini, cut in half
1 c. plain nonfat yogurt
1/2 c. brown sugar
1/4 c. vegetable oil
2 eggs or 1/2 c. liquid egg
 substitute
2 tsp. baking powder
1 tsp. baking soda
1/2 tsp. each cinnamon,
 cloves, nutmeg, and salt
1 c. flour
1 c. oatmeal
1/2 c. whole wheat flour

Preheat oven to 350° F. Spray loaf pan with nonstick cooking spray. Grate zucchini into a small bowl. In mixing bowl, combine yogurt, brown sugar and vegetable oil. Beat in eggs. Combine dry ingredients in a separate bowl and mix well. Fold dry ingredients into egg mixture and then fold in zucchini. Spoon batter into loaf pan and bake for 35 to 40 minutes. Allow bread to rest for 10 minutes, then remove from pan and cool on a wire rack.

Calories per slice: 119
Fat: 4 gm. Cholesterol: 30 mg.
Sodium: 148 mg.
For exhange diets, count: 1 bread/starch, 1 fat

Preparation time: 60 min.

OAT BRAN MUFFINS
WITH BLUEBERRIES OR RASPBERRIES
YIELD: 12 MUFFINS

★ ★ ★

1/4 c. whole wheat flour
3/4 c. white flour
1/2 c. brown sugar
1 c. oat bran cereal
4 tsp. baking powder
1/4 tsp. salt
1 c. skim milk
1 tsp. vanilla
1/3 c. liquid vegetable oil
1 egg or 1/4 c. liquid egg
    substitute
1 c. drained berries

Preheat oven to 400° F. Combine dry ingredients in a mixing bowl. Stir well. Using an egg beater, combine milk, vanilla, egg, and oil. Pour into dry ingredients and add drained blueberries or raspberries. Stir just until moistened. Spoon batter into greased or lined muffin cups and bake for 20 minutes.

Calories per muffin: 112
Fat: 6 gm. Cholesterol: 21 mg. with egg; 1 mg. with substitute
Sodium: 83 mg.
For exchange diets, count: 1 bread/starch, 1 fat

Preparation time: 40 min.

ONION CHEESE SUPPER BREAD
YIELD: 8 SLICES

★ ★ ★

1/2 c. onion, chopped
1 egg, beaten
1/2 c. skim milk
1 1/2 c. biscuit mix
1 c. part-skim American
   cheese, shredded
2 TB. parsley, chopped

Preheat oven to 400° F. In a small mixing bowl, combine egg and milk using an egg beater. In a large mixing bowl, combine chopped onion, biscuit mix, parsley, and 1/2 of the shredded cheese. Pour liquid into the large bowl and stir just until moist. Spread dough into an 8-inch round pan that has been sprayed with nonstick cooking spray. Spread remaining cheese over the top. Bake for 20 minutes.

Calories per 1 slice: 135
Fat: 6 gm. Cholesterol: 42 mg. with egg; 20 mg. with substitute
Sodium: 222 mg.
For exchange diets, count: 1 bread/starch, 1 fat

Preparation time: 35 min.

SUMMER HERB BUTTERMILK BREAD
YIELD: 1 LOAF OR 18 SLICES

★ ★ ★

2 c. whole wheat flour
2 c. white flour
1 tsp. salt
2 tsp. sugar
1 tsp. baking soda
1 tsp. baking powder
3 TB. margarine
1 tsp. oil
1 tsp. each dried basil, sage,
    tarragon, and chives
or 2 TB. each fresh herbs
    (may substitute other
    favorite herbs)
2 c. buttermilk

Preheat oven to 375° F. In a large bowl, combine first six dry ingredients. Add margarine and work into mixture until crumbly. Put oil in small glass dish, and MICROWAVE 15 seconds. Stir in herbs. This helps to bring out the flavor. Add herbs and buttermilk to crumbly mixture and mix until well blended. Spread dough into a loaf pan that has been sprayed with liquid shortening. Bake for 35 to 45 minutes, or until the middle of the loaf is firm to the touch. Cool on a rack.

Calories per slice: 122
Fat: 3 gm. Cholesterol: 2 mg.
Sodium: 234 mg.
For exchange diets, count: 1 bread/starch, 1 fat

Preparation time: 55 min.

ANTIPASTO SALAD
YIELD: 4 1-CUP SERVINGS

★ ★ ★

1 16-oz. can artichoke hearts
   in water
2 stalks celery, sliced thin
1/2 c. sliced radishes
1 TB. chopped red onion
1 small head Boston lettuce
1/4 c. reduced-calorie Italian
   dressing

Wash and drain lettuce, then tear into bite-sized pieces. Drain artichokes and combine with celery, radishes, onion, and reduced-calorie Italian salad dressing in a mixing bowl. Divide lettuce onto 4 serving plates and spoon vegetables and dressing over the top. Serve.

Calories per 1-c. serving: 68
Fat: 3 gm. Cholesterol: 1 mg.
Sodium: 191 mg.
For exchange diets, count: 3 vegetable

Preparation time: 15 min.

ASPARAGUS VINAIGRETTE
YIELD: 4 1-CUP SERVINGS

★ ★ ★

2 lb. fresh asparagus
1 onion, chopped fine
1/4 tsp. garlic powder
1/2 tsp. salt, optional
1 1/2 tsp. Dijon mustard
2 TB. lemon juice
1 TB. vegetable oil
1 tsp. red wine
1/2 tsp. vinegar
1/4 c. chopped fresh parsley

Trim and wash asparagus, then steam in MICROWAVE with 1 TB. water in a covered microwave dish on high power for 5 minutes. Place spears in a flat shallow serving dish and sprinkle with finely chopped onion. Combine all other ingredients except parsley in a blender container and pour over the asparagus. Chill in refrigerator for 20 minutes, garnish with parsley and serve.

Calories per 1-c. serving: 95
Fat: 4 gm. Cholesterol: 0
Sodium: 179 mg. with salt; 57 mg. without salt
For exchange diets, count: 2 vegetables, 1 fat

Preparation time: 40 min.

Carrot Marinade
Yield: 8 3/4-c. servings

★ ★ ★

1 1/2 lb. carrots, cut into coins
1/2 green pepper, chopped fine
1 scallion, sliced fine
8-oz. no added salt tomato
   sauce
1/4 c. vinegar
1 TB. Worcestershire sauce
2 TB. brown sugar
1 tsp. prepared mustard
1/2 tsp. celery seed

Place sliced carrots and 1 TB. water in microwave-safe 2-quart dish. Cover with plastic wrap and MICROWAVE on high for 3 minutes. Drain well. Transfer carrots to a 2-qt. salad bowl. Add green pepper and scallion. Combine tomato sauce, vinegar, brown sugar, mustard, Worcestershire sauce, and celery seed in a shaker container and pour over vegetables, tossing to coat. This salad keeps well in the refrigerator for 4 days.

Calories per 3/4-c. serving: 77
Fat: less than 1 gm. Cholesterol: 0
Sodium: 71 mg.
For exchange diets, count: 1 bread/starch

Preparation time: 20 min.

CREAMY CUCUMBER SALAD DRESSING
YIELD: 8 2-TB. SERVINGS

★ ★ ★

1/2 c. cucumber, coarsely
   chopped
1 TB. minced fresh dill
1/2 tsp. white pepper
1/2 tsp. garlic powder
1 TB. lemon juice
3/4 c. nonfat yogurt
1 TB. vegetable oil
1/4 tsp. salt
1 tsp. sugar

Using a blender, combine cucumber, dill, pepper, and garlic and
blend until creamy. Transfer to a mixing bowl and fold in
remaining ingredients; refrigerate until ready to serve. This
dressing keeps well in the refrigerator for 4 days.

Calories per 2-TB. serving: 31
Fat: 2 gm. Cholesterol: less than 1 mg.
Sodium: 83 mg.
For exchange diets, count: 1 vegetable

Preparation time: 15 min.

CUCUMBER AND LEEK SALAD
YIELD: 4 1-CUP SERVINGS

★ ★ ★

> 2 med. cucumbers, sliced thin
> 1 c. thinly sliced leeks
> 1/2 c. halved cherry tomatoes
> 2 TB. vegetable oil
> 1 TB. lemon juice
> 1/4 tsp. dried tarragon
> 1/8 tsp. white pepper
> 1/8 tsp. salt (optional)

Place cucumbers, leeks, and tomatoes in 2-quart salad bowl.
Combine oil, lemon juice, tarragon, white pepper, and optional
salt in shaker container. Shake to mix, and pour over fresh
greens or vegetables just before serving.

Calories per 1-c. serving: 95
Fat: 7 gm. Cholesterol: 0
Sodium: 61 mg. with salt; 5 mg. without salt
For exchange diets, count: 1 vegetable, 1 1/2 fat

Preparation time: 10 min.

CUCUMBERS WITH HONEY DRESSING
YIELD: 8 3/4-C. SERVINGS

* * *

3 large cucumbers, peeled and
  sliced thin
1/2 red onion, sliced finely
1 small can mandarin
  oranges, drained well

Dressing:
3 TB. orange juice
1 TB. lemon juice
1 TB. honey
2 tsp. Dijon mustard
2 tsp. grated orange rind
1/4 tsp. salt (optional)
1 TB. vegetable oil

Combine cucumbers, onion, and oranges in a 3-quart salad bowl.
Mix ingredients for dressing in a shaker container and pour over
salad ingredients just before serving, tossing to coat.

Calories per 3/4-c. serving: 51
Fat: 2 gm. Cholesterol: 0
Sodium: 79 mg. with salt; 18 mg. without salt
For exchange diets, count: 1 vegetable, 1/2 fat

Preparation time: 15 min.

EASTER SALAD
YIELD: 8 2-C. SERVINGS

★ ★ ★

4 c. torn lettuce
4 c. torn spinach
1/4 c. sliced mushrooms
1/4 c. sliced red onion
2 c. sliced oranges
2 sl. bacon, broiled and
    crumbled

Dressing:
1/3 c. vinegar
1 TB. oil
1/2 tsp. sugar
1/4 tsp. salt, optional
1/8 tsp. dry mustard

In a large salad bowl, combine lettuce, spinach, mushrooms,
onion, oranges, and crumbled bacon. In a shaker container,
combine ingredients for dressing. Pour over salad ingredients,
mixing well and serve.

Calories per 2-c. serving: 111
Fat: 4 gm. Cholesterol: 2 mg.
Sodium: 125 mg. with salt; 64 mg. without salt
For exchange diets, count: 1/2 fruit, 1 vegetable, 1 fat

Preparation time: 20 min.

FANCY MARINATED TOMATOES
YIELD: 4 1 1/2-C. SERVINGS

★ ★ ★

4 firm, ripe tomatoes
1/4 c. snipped parsley
1/2 tsp. garlic powder
1/4 tsp. salt
1 tsp. sugar
1/4 tsp. pepper
1 TB. vegetable oil
1 TB. wine vinegar
1 tsp. Dijon-style mustard

Remove stems from the tomatoes and turn omatoes upside down.
Cut partially through each tomato vertically in 3/4-inch slices.
For each tomato, spoon 1 tsp. of parsley between the slices and
place stem-side down in a shallow serving dish. Combine
remaining ingredients and pour over tomatoes. Cover and chill
at least 30 minutes. Allow to stand at room temperature for 15
minutes before serving.

Calories per 1-tomato serving: 59
Fat: 3 gm. Cholesterol: 0
Sodium: 160 mg.
For exchange diets, count: 1 vegetable, 1 fat

Preparation time: 60 min.

HONEY OF A WALDORF SALAD
YIELD: 8 1/2-C. SERVINGS

★ ★ ★

2 c. chopped apples
1 TB. lemon juice
1/2 c. celery, finely diced
1/3 c. chopped walnuts
1/2 c. sliced green grapes
1/4 c. light mayonnaise
2 TB. honey

Combine all ingredients and stir to mix. To retard browning, sprinkle the lemon juice over the apples and stir before adding the other ingredients.

Calories per 1/2-c. serving: 120
Fat: 7 gm. Cholesterol: 2 mg.
Sodium: 25 mg.
For exchange diets, count: 1 fruit, 1 1/2 fat

Preparation time: 15 min.

LEAN BEAN SALAD
YIELD: 8 1/2-C. SERVINGS

★ ★ ★

---

1 16-oz. can garbanzo beans

1 15-oz. can French style
    green beans (no salt added)

1 small red onion, chopped

1 TB. fresh or dried parsley

1 TB. vegetable oil

1/4 c. vinegar

2 TB. sugar

1 tsp. garlic powder

1/2 tsp. black pepper

1/4 c. Parmesan cheese

Drain beans well. Combine all other ingredients in a 2-quart salad bowl. Add beans. May be chilled or served immediately. This keeps well for 5 days.

Calories per 1/2-c. serving: 118
Fat: 3 gm. Cholesterol: 2 mg.
Sodium: 58 mg.
For exchange diets, count: 1 lean meat, 1 vegetable

Preparation time: 15 min.

LEMON AND BASIL SALAD DRESSING
YIELD: 1 C. OR 16 1-TB. SERVINGS

★ ★ ★

1/3 c. lemon juice
1/2 tsp. basil
1 1/2 tsp. dry mustard
1 tsp. sugar
1/4 tsp. salt
1/4 tsp. garlic powder
1/4 tsp. pepper
1/2 c. vegetable oil

Combine all ingredients except oil in a blender or shaker container. Add oil. Store in a covered container for up to 3 weeks in the refrigerator. Use over fresh greens or raw vegetables.

Calories per 1-TB. serving: 34
Fat: 4 gm. Cholesterol: 0
Sodium: 31 mg.
For exchange diets, count: 1 fat

Preparation time: 10 min.

MARINATED MUSHROOM SALAD
YIELD: 4 1/2-C. SERVINGS

★ ★ ★

1/2 c. red wine vinegar
1/3 c. water
2 tsp. vegetable oil
1/2 tsp. garlic powder
1/2 tsp. basil
1/4 tsp. thyme
Dash cayenne pepper
12 oz. fresh musrooms,
    cleaned and sliced thin

Combine first seven ingredients in a sauce pan. Bring to a boil, then simmer for 5 minutes. Add mushrooms. Remove from heat and cover for 5 minutes. Transfer to a salad bowl. Cover. Chill for at least 30 minutes. Serve with slotted spoon. Can be made a day ahead and keeps for 3 days.

Calories per 1/2-c. serving: 49
Fat: 3 gm. Cholesterol: 0
Sodium: 15 mg.
For exchange diets, count: 1 vegetable, 1/2 fat

Preparation time: 50 min.

OLD FASHIONED CUCUMBERS
YIELD: 4 1-C. SERVINGS

★ ★ ★

> 1 quart fresh cucumbers,
>   peeled and sliced thin
> 1 medium onion, cut into
>   slices
> 1 tsp. salt
> 1/4 c. sugar
> 1/4 c. vinegar
> 1/2 tsp. celery seed

Wash and prepare cucumbers and onion and layer into a shallow bowl. Sprinkle with salt and cover with 1 tray of ice cubes. Allow to marinate for at least 30 minutes. Drain well, squeezing liquid from cucumbers. Combine vinegar, sugar, and celery seed in a shaker container. Pour over vegetables and chill at least 15 minutes. This keeps 3 days.

Calories per 1-c. serving: 73
Fat: 0 Cholesterol: 0
Sodium: 61 mg.
For exchange diets, count: 1 vegetable, 1/2 fruit

Preparation time: 55 min.

SUMMER VEGETABLE MOLD
YIELD: 8 3/4-C. SERVINGS

★ ★ ★

6 cherry tomatoes
2 pkg. sugar-free lemon
gelatin
2 c. boiling water
1 c. cold water
3 TB. vinegar
1/2 c. diced and seeded
cucumber
1/4 c. green pepper, chopped
fine
1 scallion, chopped fine

Cut cherry tomatoes in half and set them aside. Pour gelatin into a small mixing bowl. Add the boiling water and stir to dissolve the gelatin. Add cold water and vinegar. Pour 1 cup of the gelatin mixture into a 2-quart mold. Chill for 30 minutes. Add remaining vegetables to gelatin left in the bowl and chill for 1 hour. When first layer of gelatin in mold has set for 30 minutes, press 12 cherry tomato halves into the mold. Allow to set 30 minutes more. Then spoon remaining gelatin and vegetables over the tomatoes and chill for 1 more hour. Unmold by placing the mold in hot water for 30 to 45 seconds; cut into 8 slices.

Calories per 3/4 c. serving: 27
Fat: 0 Cholesterol: 0
Sodium: 8 mg.
For exchange diets, count: 1 vegetable

Preparation time: 2 hr.

Speed Alert: This recipe requires 2 hours for gelatin to set.

TWENTY CALORIE MOLDED SALAD
YIELD: 4 1-C. SERVINGS

★ ★ ★

> 1 c. boiling water
> 2 3-oz. packages sugar-free or
>   regular lemon gelatin
> 6 large ice cubes
> 1 TB. lemon juice
> 1 c. chopped celery
> 1 c. shredded cabbage and
>   carrots

Pour boiling water over gelatin in a bowl, stirring until gelatin is
dissolved. Stir in lemon juice and ice cubes and chill for 1 hour or
until mixture is thick. Stir in vegetables and transfer to an 8-
inch square pan or 1-quart salad bowl. Chill for 1 hour more and
cut into 4 servings.

Calories per serving: 22 (using sugar-free gelatin)
Fat: 0 Cholesterol: 0
Sodium: 41 mg.
For exchange diets, count: 1 vegetable

Preparation time: 2 hr.

Speed Alert: This recipe requires 2 hours for gelatin to set.

Tex Mex Slaw
Yield: 8 1-c. servings

★ ★ ★

1/2 head green cabbage
1 red onion, shredded
1 c. taco sauce
1/3 c. light mayonnaise
16 oz. can black beans,
  drained
12 oz. frozen whole kernel
  corn

Shred cabbage to desired texture. Transfer to a salad bowl.
Shred onion and add to cabbage. Steam frozen corn for 3
minutes, then drain. Combine taco sauce and light mayonnaise.
Toss cabbage, drained beans, and corn with taco sauce dressing
just before serving.

Calories per 1-c. serving: 120
Fat: 3 gm. Cholesterol: 3 mg.
Sodium: 69 mg.
For exchange diets, count: 1 vegetable, 1 fat,
1/2 bread/starch

Preparation time: 20 min.

TOMATO DRESSING
YIELD: 2 1/2 CUPS OR 10 1/4-c. SERVINGS

★ ★ ★

> 2 ripe tomatoes, chopped
> 1 stalk celery, finely chopped
> 1 carrot, grated
> 1/2 red pepper, diced
> 1/2 green pepper, diced
> 1/4 c. scallions
> 1/2 tsp. garlic powder
> 1/4 c. red wine vinegar
> 2 TB. olive oil

Combine all ingredients. Store in a covered container in the refrigerator. Stir before serving. This keeps well for 3 days. This dressing is great on pasta or fresh green salads.

Calories per 1/4-c. serving: 12
Fat: 0   Cholesterol: 0
Sodium: 118 mg.
For exchange diets, count: 1/2 vegetable

Preparation time: 15 min.

WANT MORE SALAD
YIELD: 4 3/4-c. SERVINGS

* * *

Kids love it!

2 Granny Smith apples, cut
  fine
3 stalks celery, chopped fine
1/4 c. raisins
2 TB. sunflower seeds
7 oz. pineapple chunks in
  juice, drained well

Dressing:
1/4 c. light mayonnaise
1/4 c. plain nonfat yogurt
2 TB. orange juice
2 pkg. Equal® sugar
  substitute or 2 tsp. sugar

Combine first five ingredients in a salad bowl. Combine dressing
ingredients and pour over fruits. Toss and refrigerate or serve.
This keeps well for 2 days.

Calories per 3/4 -c. serving: 155
Fat: 6 gm. Cholesterol: 11 mg.
Sodium: 155 mg.
For exchange diets, count: 1 fat, 1 1/2 fruit

Preparation time: 20 min.

ASPARAGUS CHEF SALAD
YIELD: 4 1-C. SERVINGS

★ ★ ★

2 1/2 lb. asparagus, trimmed
8 oz. mushrooms, sliced
2 oz. part-skim julienne Swiss
cheese
2 oz. lean julienne ham
1 TB. finely chopped onion
1 orange, peeled and cubed

Dressing:
1 pkg. lemon and herb salad
dressing mix
2 TB. water
1/4 c. vinegar
1/4 c. vegetable oil

Chop asparagus into bite-sized pieces and place in a microwave-proof casserole dish. Add 2 TB. water, cover, and MICROWAVE for 2 minutes. Drain. Measure remaining ingredients into a salad bowl. Add asparagus when completely cool. Prepare dressing in a shaker container and add approximately 1/3 of it to the salad. Save remaining dressing for greens and fresh vegetables.

Calories per 1-c. serving: 151
Fat: 5 gm. Cholesterol: 25 mg.
Sodium: 347 mg.
For exchange diets, count: 2 vegetable,
1 lean meat, 1 fat

Preparation time: 35 min.

BAKED BURRITO
YIELD: 8 8-OZ. SERVINGS

★ ★ ★

8 10-inch flour tortillas
1 lb. lean ground beef
4 oz. part-skim American
  cheese
1/4 c. chopped scallions

Mexican Sauce:
8 oz. no added salt tomato
  sauce
1/4 tsp. garlic powder
1/2 tsp. cumin
1/8 tsp. cayenne powder
  (optional)
1/2 tsp. dried jalapeno
  peppers (optional)
1 TB. lemon juice
1 TB. sugar

Brown and drain the ground beef. Meanwhile, shred the cheese
and chop the onions. Mix the sauce ingredients together and
pour over drained beef, stirring to mix. Place 1/2 c. beef in each
tortilla, fold and place seam side down on a baking sheet. Top
with cheese and scallions. Bake 15 minutes at 350° F. Serve
with lettuce and tomatoes. These burritos freeze well on sheets
or in baking dishes.

Calories per 1 serving: 212
Fat: 6 gm. Cholesterol: 57 mg.
Sodium: 180 mg.
For exchange diets, count: 2 lean meat,
1 bread/starch, 1 vegetable

Preparation time: 35 min.

BAYOU FISH STEW
YIELD: 4 1 1/2-c. SERVINGS

★ ★ ★

If you've never tried fish stew, you're in for a special discovery!

> 1 lb. white fish, thawed
> (haddock, cod, or trout are
> great)
>
> 2 scallions, chopped
>
> 4 oz. fresh mushrooms, sliced
>
> 1 small zucchini, sliced
>
> 1 green pepper, chopped
>
> 12 oz. chunky tomatoes
>
> 1 c. quick rice
>
> 1/2 tsp. each garlic powder
> and cumin
>
> Cayenne to taste
>
> 8 oz. no added salt tomato
> sauce
>
> 1 tsp. each basil and
> Worcestershire sauce

Steam fish with 1 TB. water in the MICROWAVE for 3 minutes.
Cool and cube into small pieces. Saute onions, mushrooms,
zucchini and pepper in the bottom of a dutch oven that has been
sprayed with nonstick cooking spray. Add fish and all remaining
ingredients to vegetables in Dutch oven and simmer for 30
minutes. Or MICROWAVE uncovered in a 3-quart casserole dish
for 15 minutes.

Calories per 1 1/2-c. serving: 320
Fat: 8 gm. Cholesterol: 62 mg.
Sodium: 40 mg.
For exchange diets, count: 3 lean meat, 2 vegetable,1 bread/starch

Preparation time: 40 min.

111

BEAN CASSEROLE OLE´
YIELD: 8 1 1/2-C. SERVINGS

★ ★ ★

4 strips bacon, broiled crisp

2 TB. margarine

1 c. chopped onion

1 green pepper, diced

4 tsp. chili powder

1 tsp. garlic powder

1 tsp. dried jalapeno pepper
(optional)

2 15-oz. cans pinto or kidney
beans

1 14-oz. can chopped tomatoes
or 2 c. fresh tomatoes

1/2 c. shredded part-skim
American cheese

1/2 c. shredded part-skim
Monterey jack cheese

Broil bacon until crisp and crumble. Set aside. Saute onion and pepper in the margarine in a skillet. Combine the sauteed vegetables, beans, seasonings and tomatoes in a 3-quart baking dish. Stir well. Bake for 35 minutes at 350° F. Sprinkle with cheese and bacon and bake for 5 more minutes. Serve. Leftovers freeze well.

Calories per 1 1/2-c. serving: 349
Fat: 11 gm. Cholesterol: 28 mg.
Sodium: 392 mg.
For exchange diets, count: 2 meat, 2 bread/starch, 1 fat, 1 vegetable

Preparation time: 55 min.

BROCCOLI AND CHEESE ENCHILADAS
YIELD: 8 SERVINGS

★ ★ ★

1 medium onion, chopped
1 TB. margarine
1 10-oz. pkg. frozen spinach,
  thawed and squeezed dry
4 oz. part-skim mozzarella
  cheese
1 c. part-skim Ricotta cheese
2 c. frozen broccoli, thawed
1/2 c. picante sauce
1 tsp. cumin
1/4 tsp. garlic powder
8 flour tortillas

Saute onion in margarine until tender. Meanwhile,
MICROWAVE spinach and broccoli 3 minutes on high power to
thaw. Drain well. In mixing bowl, combine onion, vegetables,
1/2 c. of mozzarella cheese, Ricotta cheese, picante sauce, cumin,
and garlic powder. Spoon 1/2 c. filling onto each tortilla and roll
up. Place seam side down in a baking dish that has been sprayed
with nonstick cooking spray. Top with remaining mozzarella
cheese. Bake at 350° F. for 20 minutes. Serve with shredded
lettuce and tomatoes.

Calories per serving: 212
Fat: 8 gm. Cholesterol: 17 mg.
Sodium: 348 mg. (To reduce sodium, use no added salt tomato sauce
instead of picante sauce.)
For exchange diets, count: 2 meat, 1 vegetable, 1 bread/starch

Preparation time: 40 min.

Chicken Chestnut Salad
Yield: 4 1-c. servings

★ ★ ★

2 c. chunked white meat of
chicken (or turkey)

1/2 c. peeled and chopped
cucumber

1/2 c. diced celery

1/2 c. water chestnuts,
drained and sliced

1/4 c. each diced green
pepper, scallions and
pimento

1/4 c. light mayonnaise

Salad greens of choice

Paprika for garnish

Toss first seven ingredients with mayonnaise. Serve on fresh
greens and garnish with paprika.

Calories per 1-c. serving: 146
Fat: 9 gm. Cholesterol: 36 mg.
Sodium: 153 mg.
For exchange diets, count: 2 lean meat,
2 vegetable

Preparation time: 15 min.

CURRIED CHICKEN SALAD
YIELD: 4 2-C. SERVINGS

★ ★ ★

1/2 c. plain yogurt

1 TB. each peanut butter and
sugar

2 TB. skim milk

2 tsp. curry powder

6 c. torn mixed greens

2 c. diced cooked chicken

1 c. each shredded green
cabbage and red cabbage

11 oz. mandarin oranges,
drained well

1 oz. peanuts, chopped

1 TB. chopped scallions

Combine yogurt, peanut butter, milk, sugar, and curry in a
shaker container. In a salad bowl, arrange greens, chicken,
cabbages, oranges, peanuts, and scallions. Toss salad with
dressing, serve.

Calories per 2-c. serving: 282
Fat: 12 gm. Cholesterol: 52 mg.
Sodium: 85 mg.
For exchange diets, count: 3 lean meat, 1 fat, 1 bread/starch

Preparation time: 20 min.

DEEP DISH PIZZA
YIELD: 12 SLICES

★ ★ ★

1 lb. loaf frozen white or
  wheat bread dough

1 TB. vegetable oil

8 oz. part-skim mozzarella
  cheese, shredded

8 oz. lean ground pork,
  browned

1/2 c. each chopped onion and
  green pepper

8 oz. no added salt tomato
  sauce

1/2 tsp. each garlic powder
  and fennel

1/4 tsp. pepper

1 tsp. each basil and oregano

1/2 tsp. sugar

Thaw frozen dough the day before in the refrigerator or oven-
thaw. (To oven-thaw, preheat the oven to 200° F. Turn off oven.
Place oiled bread dough in oiled 15 x 8-inch or 12-inch round pan.
Cover with a towel and leave for 45 minutes in the preheated
oven.) Work thawed dough to the edges and part way up the
sides of the pan. Sprinkle first with cheese, then pork, onions,
and pepper. Combine tomato sauce with seasonings and pour
over all. Bake at 450° F. for 40 minutes or until edges are
browned and the middle has risen. Remove from oven and allow
to stand for 10 minutes. Cut and serve. Freeze or refrigerate
leftovers.

Calories per 1-slice serving: 229
Fat: 10 gm. Cholesterol: 22 mg.
Sodium: 293 mg.
For exchange diets, count: 2 lean meat, 1 1/2 bread/starch, 1 fat

Preparation time: 60 min.

EASY SEAFOOD SALAD
YIELD: 4 1-C. SERVINGS

★ ★ ★

1 c. salad shrimp, cooked
1 c. crab or flaked mock crab
1/2 c. chopped celery
1/4 c. chopped pimiento
2 TB. minced onion
1 c. green peas, thawed
1/2 c. reduced-calorie 1000
  Island dressing
1 tsp. lemon juice
1/4 tsp. pepper
1/4 tsp. marjoram
1/4 c. plain nonfat yogurt

Combine shrimp, crab, celery, pimiento, and onion in a serving
bowl. In shaker container, mix salad dressing, lemon juice,
pepper, marjoram, and yogurt. Pour dressing over salad, toss,
and serve.

Calories per 1-c. serving: 154
Fat: 4 gm. Cholesterol: 63 mg.
Sodium: 388 mg.
For exchange diets, count: 1 bread/starch,
1 1/2 lean meat

Preparation time: 15 min.

EGGS FOR A BUNCH

YIELD: 8 3-INCH SQUARES

★ ★ ★

12 slices of white or French
   bread, crusts removed

4 oz. lean cubed ham

2 c. skim milk

8 eggs or 2 c. liquid egg
   substitute

1/4 c. minced onion

1/2 tsp. dry mustard

1/4 tsp. paprika

1/4 tsp. salt

1 TB. dried parsley

Cut bread into cubes and spread over the bottom of a 7 x 11-inch or 9 x 12-inch pan that has been sprayed with nonstick cooking spray. Sprinkle ham on top of bread. Using a mixer or blender, combine milk, eggs, onion, mustard, paprika, and salt. Pour over ham. Sprinkle with parsley. Bake at 400° F. for 35-40 minutes or refrigerate overnight and then bake in the morning. Perfect for brunch.

Calories per 3-inch square: 245
Fat: 7 gm. Cholesterol: 266 mg. with eggs; 15 mg. with substitute
Sodium: 377 mg.
For exchange diets, count: 2 lean meat,
1 1/2 bread/starch

Preparation time: 60 min.

FILLING SPINACH SALAD
YIELD: 4 1-C. SERVINGS

★ ★ ★

---

1 lb. freshly chopped spinach
4 oz. lean ham, diced
4 oz. Farmer's cheese,
  shredded
1/2 c. sliced scallions
1 10-oz. pkg. frozen peas,
  thawed
Dressing:
2 TB. light mayonnaise
1/4 c. light sour cream
1/2 c. nonfat yogurt
2 tsp. Worcestershire sauce
1 tsp. lemon juice
1/2 tsp. white pepper

Combine spinach, ham, cheese, scallions, and peas in a salad
bowl. In a small bowl, whisk together ingredients for dressing.
Pour dressing over salad just before serving.

Calories per 2 c. serving: 228
Fat: 9 gm. Cholesterol: 33 mg.
Sodium: 636 mg.
For exchange diets, count: 2 lean meat,
3 vegetables, 1 fat

Preparation time: 15 min.

NUTRITION ALERT: This recipe is high in sodium. It is
intended for occasional use only. Substitute turkey for ham to
reduce the sodium.

GARDEN PIZZA
YIELD: 8 SLICES

★ ★ ★

1 Robin Hood Pizza Crust Mix, prepared according to package directions
2 c. sliced mushrooms
1 1/2 c. shredded carrots
1/2 c. chopped onions
1 c. finely sliced zucchini
1 TB. vegetable oil
8 oz. no added salt tomato sauce
1/4 tsp. each garlic and fennel
1 tsp. each basil and oregano
1 tsp. brown sugar
1 c. part-skim mozzarella cheese
1/2 c. Parmesan cheese

Preheat oven to 425° F. Spray a 14-inch round pizza crisper pan with nonstick cooking spray. Press prepared crust onto pan. Bake for 14 to 16 minutes. Meanwhile, saute mushrooms, carrots, zucchini and onion in oil over medium heat for 3 minutes. When crust is prebaked, sprinkle with vegetables, sauce, seasonings, and two kinds of cheese. Bake for 15 more minutes. Remove from oven; cool for 3 minutes before slicing.

This recipe may be easily frozen after fully prepared. To use later, thaw at room temperature, place on a pizza crisper pan, and heat at 300° F. for 15 minutes.

Calories per slice: 190
Fat: 7 gm. Cholesterol: 12 mg.
Sodium: 245 mg.
For exchange diets, count: 1 bread/starch,
1 1/2 lean meat, 1 vegetable

Preparation time: 40 min.

HOT CRAB WITH VEGETABLES
YIELD: 8 1 1/2-C. SERVINGS

★ ★ ★

6 medium tomatoes
1 c. evaporated skim milk
2 TB. margarine
2 TB. lemon juice
1/8 tsp. nutmeg
1/4 tsp. salt
1/2 tsp. pepper
2 c. or 16 oz. imitation crab
1/4 lb. mushrooms
1/2 c. frozen peas
1/2 c. vegetable spiral pasta
1/4 c. Parmesan cheese

Skin, chop, and cook tomatoes for 5 minutes. Add evaporated skim milk and margarine and cook for 10 minutes. Add lemon juice, nutmeg, salt, and pepper. Stir in crab and remove from heat. Meanwhile, steam mushrooms and peas. Cook spiral pasta for 8 minutes in boiling water. Drain the pasta. Mix crab into the sauce; then combine with pasta and vegetables in a large serving bowl. Sprinkle with cheese and serve.

Calories per 1-c. serving: 382
Fat: 11 gm. Cholesterol: 65 mg.
Sodium: 336 mg. with salt; 214 mg. without salt
For exchange diets, count: 4 lean meat,
2 bread/starch

Preparation time: 25 min.

CINDY'S LASAGNA SALAD
YIELD: 4 8-OZ. SERVINGS

★ ★ ★

8 lasagna noodles, cooked and drained

1 TB. vegetable oil

1 c. low-fat cottage cheese

2 oz. shredded mozzarella cheese

16 fresh spinach leaves, chopped

1/2 tsp. garlic powder

1 tsp. basil

1/4 tsp. black pepper

1 c. chopped tomatoes

1/2 c. low-calorie Italian dressing

Brush cooked noodles with oil. Combine cheeses, spinach, and garlic. Spread cheese mixture over noodles. Season with basil and pepper. Roll up noodles. Place on serving platter. Sprinkle with chopped tomatoes and your choice of low-calorie Italian dressing.

Calories per 2 noodle serving: 325
Fat: 10 gm. Cholesterol: 17 mg.
Sodium: 291 mg.
For exchange diets, count: 3 lean meat,
2 bread/starch

Preparation time: 20 min.

LAYERED SUMMER SALAD
YIELD: 4 1 1/2-C. SERVINGS

★ ★ ★

3 c. shredded lettuce or fresh
greens of choice

1/2 c. low-calorie buttermilk
dressing

2 strips of bacon, broiled and
crumbled

2 c. cherry tomatoes, halved

2 oz. cubed part-skim
mozzarella cheese

8 oz. turkey or chicken,
cooked and cubed

In a 3-quart salad bowl, layer the ingredients as follows: lettuce,
1/4 c. dressing, bacon, tomatoes, cheese, turkey or chicken, and
remaining 1/4 c. of dressing. Serve immediately or refrigerate
overnight.

Calories per 1 1/2-c. serving: 208
Fat: 8 gm. Cholesterol: 57 mg.
Sodium: 637
For exchange diets, count: 3 lean meat,
1 vegetable

Preparation time: 20 min.

Nutrition alert: This recipe is high in sodium. Reduce the
sodium by omitting bacon, and by using low-sodium cheese.

MEDITERRANEAN SUPPER
YIELD: 8 1-C. SERVINGS

★ ★ ★

1 1/2 lb. lean ground beef	1 tsp. oregano
1/2 c. each diced green pepper, celery, and onion	6 oz. no added salt tomato paste
1/2 tsp. each garlic powder and black pepper	3 c. water
1/4 tsp. salt (optional)	1 c. bread crumbs
2 c. diced eggplant or zucchini	1/4 c. Parmesan cheese
2 TB. dried parsley	1 tsp. margarine
1 c. uncooked quick rice	2 TB. sliced green olives

Preheat oven to 450° F. Brown ground beef in a large skillet and drain well. Add pepper, celery, onion, and garlic, cooking until vegetables are tender. Stir in salt, pepper, eggplant or zucchini, parsley, rice, oregano, tomato paste, and water. Bring to a boil, then simmer 20 minutes, covered. Pour into a 3-quart baking dish. Sprinkle with sliced olives, bread crumbs, and Parmesan cheese and dot with margarine. Bake for 15 minutes or MICROWAVE on high power for 8 to 10 minutes until cheese and margarine are melted and crumbs are browned. This recipe may be fully baked, then frozen.

Calories per 1-c. serving: 274
Fat: 12 gm. Cholesterol: 72 mg.
Sodium: 423 mg. with salt; 362 without salt
For exchange diets, count: 3 lean meat,
1 bread/starch, 1/2 fat

Preparation time: 45 min.

MEXICAN TURKEY SALAD
YIELD: 4 1 1/2-C. SERVINGS

★ ★ ★

1 c. quick rice
1 c. water
1 ripe tomato, diced
1 green pepper, chopped
2 c. cooked turkey
2 TB. green chilis

Dressing:
1/2 c. nonfat yogurt
1 TB. vegetable oil
1 1/2 tsp. chili powder
1/2 tsp. each cumin and sugar
1/4 tsp. garlic powder
1/4 tsp. salt (optional)

Combine rice and water in 1-quart microwave dish, cover tightly, and MICROWAVE on high for 3 minutes. Meanwhile, prepare vegetables. When rice is cooked, rinse quickly with cold water and transfer to colander to drain. In salad bowl, combine vegetables, turkey, and rice. In shaker container, blend ingredients for dressing, and pour over salad just before serving.

This recipe may be easily doubled. If using for a meal several days later, simply combine the turkey, rice and vegetables in a covered plastic container and mix with dressing just before serving.

Calories per 1 1/2-c. serving: 248
Fat: 5 gm. Cholesterol: 35 mg.
Sodium: 130 mg. with salt, 58 mg. without salt
For exchange diets, count: 1 1/2 bread/starch, 2 lean meat, 1 vegetable

Preparation time: 20 min.

PIZZA SALAD
YIELD: 4 1 1/2-c. SERVINGS

★ ★ ★

4 c. chopped fresh lettuce or
   greens
2 lg. tomatoes, cut into
   wedges
8 large mushrooms, sliced
4 oz. part-skim mozzarella
   cheese, shredded
1/2 c. diced lean ham
1 TB. vegetable oil
1/4 c. red wine vinegar
1/4 tsp. sugar
1 TB. Italian spice blend

Layer lettuce, tomato, mushrooms, cheese, and ham on salad plates. Combine vegetable oil, red wine vinegar, sugar, and spices in a shaker container. Shake dressing over salad and serve.

Calories per serving: 161
Fat: 11 gm. Cholesterol: 22 mg.
Sodium: 349 mg.
For exchange diets, count: 2 lean meat, 1 vegetable,
1 fat

Preparation time: 15 min.

PORK AND BLACK BEAN STIR-FRY
YIELD: 8 1 1/2-C. SERVINGS

★ ★ ★

1 tsp. vegetable oil

1 lb. lean pork (such as loin), cut into strips

2 TB. chili powder

1 small onion

1/4 tsp. garlic powder

16-oz. can black beans, drained

1 pt. cherry tomatoes, cut in half

1 c. frozen corn, thawed

1 TB. lemon juice

1/4 tsp. salt, optional

Heat oil in large skillet over medium heat. Stir-fry pork with chili powder until pork is browned and cooked through, about 3 minutes. Set pork aside. Add onion and garlic to the pan and stir-fry for 1 minute. Add remaining ingredients and stir-fry for 3 more minutes. Stir in pork, heat through, and serve.

Leftovers may be frozen for a later meal. Reheat in the microwave.

Calories per 12 oz. serving: 270
Fat: 8 gm. Cholesterol: 59 mg.
Sodium: 45 mg. without salt; 112 mg. with salt
For exchange diets, count: 1 vegetable,
1 bread/starch, 3 lean meat

Preparation time: 15 min.

SEAFOOD AND SUMMER VEGETABLES
YIELD: 4 2-C. SERVINGS

⋆ ⋆ ⋆

1 TB. vegetable oil

4 small red-skinned potatoes

1/2 red onion

1/2 tsp. each white pepper and thyme

1/4 tsp. garlic powder

1/4 tsp. salt (optional)

4 lemon slices

1 lb. perch or haddock, thawed

1 zucchini, sliced thin

1 green pepper, chopped and 1 tomato, chopped

1/4 c. white wine

Preheat oven to 375° F. In skillet, heat oil and add sliced potatoes, sliced onion, garlic, thyme, salt, and pepper. Cover and cook 15 minutes, stirring occasionally. Meanwhile, place lemon slices in a 9 x 9-inch baking dish. Place fish over lemon and top with sliced zucchini, green pepper, and tomato. Pour on wine. Spoon potato mixture with liquid over tomatoes. Cover and bake for 25 minutes or MICROWAVE the covered dish at 70% power for 11 to 12 minutes until vegetables are tender.

Calories per 3-oz. fish and 1 c. vegetable serving: 272
Fat: 8 gm. Cholesterol: 68 mg.
Sodium: 226 mg. with salt; 104 mg. without salt.
For exchange diets, count: 1 bread/starch,
3 lean meat, 1 vegetable

Preparation time: 35 min.

SHRIMP CASSEROLE
YIELD: 4 1 1/2-C. SERVINGS

★ ★ ★

2 TB. margarine
1/2 c. celery, chopped
1 c. onions, chopped
1/4 tsp. celery seed
1 16-oz. can chopped tomatoes
1/4 c. ketchup
2 tsp. horseradish
2 tsp. Worcestershire sauce
Red pepper sauce as desired
1/2 c. soda cracker crumbs,
    crushed
1 beaten egg or 1/4 c. liquid
    egg substitute
1 lb. shrimp, thawed
1 tsp. dried parsley

Preheat oven to 375° F. Saute celery and onion in margarine in 2-quart Dutch oven. Stir in all remaining ingredients and transfer to a shallow 2-quart casserole dish sprayed with nonstick cooking spray. Bake for 25 minutes or MICROWAVE 12 to 15 minutes until mixture is evenly browned and thickened.

Calories per 1 1/2-c. serving: 255
Fat: 9 gm. Cholesterol: 214 mg. with egg; 150 mg. with substitute
Sodium: 436 mg.
For exchange diets, count: 3 lean meat, 1 1/2 bread/starch

Preparation time: 45 min.

SPRING TURKEY SALAD
YIELD: 4 1 1/2-C. SERVINGS

★ ★ ★

1/4 c. light mayonnaise
2 TB. honey
1/4 tsp. ginger
1/2 c. diced celery
2 c. chopped turkey
1 11-oz. can mandarin
    oranges, drained
1 c. chopped apple
1 c. grape halves
8 oz. pineapple chunks,
    drained

In a serving bowl, combine mayonnaise, honey, and ginger, mixing well. Add remaining ingredients and mix lightly. Chill or serve.

Calories per 1 1/2-c. serving: 243
Fat: 6 gm. Cholesterol: 47 mg.
Sodium: 70 mg.
For exchange diets, count: 2 fruit, 2 lean meat

Preparation time: 20 min.

TURKEY ROLL-UPS
YIELD: 4 8-OZ. SERVINGS

★ ★ ★

This cold entree is perfect for summer evenings.

12 broccoli spears, steamed
24 carrot sticks, steamed
12 slices turkey breast
   (approx. 1 lb.)
1 TB. vegetable oil
2 TB. white wine vinegar
2 TB. sesame seeds
1/4 tsp. pepper
1/4 tsp. salt (optional)
1 tsp. sugar

Wash and prepare carrots and broccoli for steaming. Steam with 1 TB. water in covered dish in the MICROWAVE for 4 minutes. Drain. Chill. Wrap 1 slice of turkey around a bundle of 2 carrot sticks and 1 spear of broccoli, placing seam side down in a serving dish. Chill for at least 15 min. Combine oil, vinegar, sesame seeds, salt, sugar, and pepper in shaker container. Pour over turkey roll-ups just before serving.

Calories per 3 roll-up serving: 305
Fat: 6 gm.   Cholesterol: 73 mg.
Sodium: 280 mg. with salt; 158 mg. without salt
For exchange diets, count: 1 bread/starch, 3 lean meat, 2 vegetable

Preparation time: 45 min.

ZUCCHINI LASAGNE CASSEROLE
YIELD: 4 1 1/2-c. SERVINGS

★ ★ ★

1 lb. lean ground beef, browned and drained	8 oz. no added salt tomato sauce
4 small zucchini, peeled and sliced thin lengthwise	1/4 tsp. each garlic powder, fennel, and pepper
1 onion, chopped	1 tsp. each basil and oregano
1 green pepper, chopped	2 oz. mozzarella cheese, shredded
4 oz. mushrooms, sliced	2/3 c. low-fat cottage cheese
1/2 tsp. vegetable oil	1/3 c. Parmesan cheese

Preheat oven to 375° F. (Recipe can be microwaved.) Saute onion, pepper and mushrooms in oil in dutch oven or MICROWAVE 4 minutes in 2-quart casserole dish. Meanwhile, steam sliced zucchini 6 minutes on stove top or MICROWAVE with 1 TB. water for 3 minutes in covered container. Stir meat, tomato sauce, and seasonings into sauteed vegetables. Combine cottage and mozzarella cheeses in separate bowl. Spray an 8-inch square baking dish with nonstick cooking spray. Layer zucchini, cheeses, and meat sauce twice. Sprinkle Parmesan cheese over last meat layer. Bake for 45 minutes or MICROWAVE 20 minutes. This can be assembled and frozen for later use.

Calories per 1 1/2-c. serving: 298
Fat: 9 gm. Cholesterol: 77 mg.
Sodium: 421 mg.
For exchange diets, count: 3 lean meat, 1 skim milk, 2 vegetable

Preparation time: 55 min. using microwave method

BROILED SALMON STEAKS
YIELD: 4 4-OZ. SERVINGS

★ ★ ★

---

1 lb. salmon steaks, thawed
(may substitute halibut or
cod)
1 TB. fresh chives, chopped
1/4 tsp. pepper
1 TB. lemon juice
1/4 tsp. marjoram

Place salmon steak on baking sheet which has been sprayed with nonstick cooking spray. Sprinkle remaining ingredients over fish. Broil over medium flame for 20 minutes or until salmon flakes with a fork. For MICROWAVE, cook uncovered for 6 minutes.

Calories per 4-oz. serving: 220
Fat: 7 gm. Cholesterol: 35 mg.
Sodium: 45 mg.
For exchange diets, count: 4 lean meat

Preparation time: 15 min.

CAJUN FISH ON THE GRILL
YIELD: 4 4-OZ. SERVINGS

★ ★ ★

1 lb. firm white fish of choice

1 tsp. Cajun or Creole seasoning
(use a commercial seasoning
blend or see recipe on page
141)

Spray shortening

2 TB. lemon juice

1 TB. fresh minced basil or 1 tsp.
dried basil

Thaw fillets. Cover grate of grill with aluminum foil. Spray foil
with liquid shortening. Sprinkle 1/2 tsp. seasoning over foil. Place
fillets over seasoning. Grill for 5 minutes. Sprinkle tops of fish with
remaining seasoning. Turn fillets. Grill for 5 to 10 more minutes,
depending on thickness of fillets. Dot with lemon juice and sprinkle
with basil just before serving.

Calories per 4-oz. serving: 220
Fat: 4 gm. Cholesterol: 72 mg.
Sodium: With sodium-free Cajun seasoning, 71 mg. (Check sodium content
of seasoning. This will vary.)
For exchange diets, count: 4 lean meat

Preparation time: 15 min.

CHICKEN DIVAN
YIELD: 4 1-C. SERVINGS

★ ★ ★

1 lg. bunch broccoli
1 lb. skinned chicken pieces
  or 4 skinned breasts
1 c. quick rice
1 no added salt chicken broth
1 c. nonfat plain yogurt
2 TB. reduced-calorie
  mayonnaise
1 TB. flour
1 TB. lemon juice
1 tsp. curry powder
Fresh parsley for garnish

Preheat oven to 375° F. (Recipe can be microwaved.) Wash
broccoli and cut off the full spears. MICROWAVE spears in 1 TB.
water in covered microwave dish until color changes (about 3
minutes). Drain. In same dish, combine chicken, rice, and broth.
MICROWAVE covered for 8 minutes. In the meantime, combine
yogurt, mayonnaise, flour, lemon juice, and curry powder in a
small bowl. When chicken and rice are done, place broccoli
spears on top. Pour curry dressing over broccoli. Cover. Bake for
15 minutes or MICROWAVE for 8 minutes. Serve.

Calories per 1-c. serving: 358
Fat: 8 gm. Cholesterol: 89 mg.
Sodium: 277 mg.
For exchange diets, count: 1 bread/starch, 3 lean meat, 2 vegetable, 1/2
skim milk

Preparation time: 35 min.

CORNFLAKE CHICKEN OR FISH
YIELD: 4 3-OZ. SERVINGS

★ ★ ★

2 egg whites, whipped
1 1/2 c. evaporated skim milk
1 tsp. poultry seasoning
3 c. crushed cornflakes
1 lb. chicken, skinned, in
  pieces, or 1 lb. frozen fish
  fillets

Preheat oven to 400° F. Combine egg whites, milk, and seasoning in a mixing bowl. Whip for 2 minutes. Meanwhile, crush cornflakes in a plastic bag. Dip chicken or fish in milk, then shake in cornflakes and place on a baking sheet. For chicken, bake for 35 to 45 minutes. For fish, reduce time to 15 to 20 minutes.

Calories per 3-oz. serving: 215
Fat: 9 gm. Cholesterol: 66 mg.
Sodium: 230 mg.
For exchange diets, count: 3 lean meat,
1/2 bread/starch

Preparation time: 35 min. for fish; 55 min. for chicken

FANCY RED SNAPPER
YIELD: 4 4-OZ. SERVINGS

★ ★ ★

1 lb. red snapper fillets
1/4 c. white wine
1/2 tsp. garlic powder
1 tsp. dried basil
1 TB. lemon juice
1 tsp. Worcestershire sauce
1 TB. vegetable oil
1/4 c. flour
Pepper to taste

Preheat oven to 375° F. In shallow dish, lightly dust fillets in flour. In skillet, saute fillets in 1 TB. oil until brown. Place in baking dish. Sprinkle with pepper and bake for 10 minutes or until nearly done. Meanwhile, combine all remaining ingredients in skillet. Bring to a simmer, then add baked fillets. Cook for 1 to 2 minutes and serve. Garnish with fresh parsley or tarragon.

Calories per 4-oz. serving: 164
Fat: 4 gm. Cholesterol: 60 mg.
Sodium: 79 mg.
For exchange diets, count: 3 lean meat

Preparation time: 25 min.

GOURMET CHICKEN WITH CHEESE
YIELD: 4 4-OZ. SERVINGS

★ ★ ★

1/2 c. part-skim Ricotta cheese
1/4 c. shredded part-skim
mozzarella cheese
4 TB. Parmesan cheese
1 TB. bread crumbs
1/2 tsp. basil
2 chicken breasts, split and
boned

Preheat oven to 350° F. Combine Ricotta, mozzarella, 2 TB. Parmesan, bread crumbs, and basil in a small bowl. Carefully separate skin from flesh of each chicken breast, leaving one side of skin attached. Spoon half of cheese mixture between skin and flesh of each breast half. Pull skin edges under breast; secure with wooden toothpicks. Place chicken, skin side up, in shallow baking pan. Bake uncovered until chicken is cooked through and golden brown, about 35 minutes. Sprinkle with remaining Parmesan cheese. Serve.

To save calories, cholesterol, and fat, do not eat the skin. The chicken can be prepared, stuffed, and frozen.

Calories per 4-oz. serving: 275
Fat: 10 gm. Cholesterol: 95 mg.
Sodium: 306 mg.
For exchange diets, count: 1 skim milk, 4 lean meat

Preparation time: 50 min.

LEMON CHICKEN FOR COMPANY
YIELD: 4 4-OZ. SERVINGS

★ ★ ★

4 boned and skinned chicken
 breasts
Juice of 1 lemon
1 TB. vegetable oil
1/2 c. flour
1/4 tsp. salt
1/2 tsp. paprika
1/4 tsp. pepper
1 TB. grated lemon peel
2 TB. brown sugar
1 TB. water
1 lemon, sliced thin

Place chicken breasts in a flat pan and cover with fresh lemon juice, reserving 1 TB. for later use. Cover and marinate in the refrigerator for at least 20 minutes. Next, preheat oven to 425° F. Pour oil in a shallow baking pan and place in the oven until it heats up. Meanwhile, combine flour, salt, paprika, and pepper in a plastic bag. Remove chicken from marinade and place it in the plastic bag, shaking to coat. Lower oven to 350° F., and place chicken on baking pan with heated oil. Mix grated lemon peel with the brown sugar and sprinkle over chicken. Combine water and 1 TB. reserved lemon juice and sprinkle over chicken. Slice fresh lemon and place one slice on each breast. Bake uncovered for 35 to 40 minutes.

Calories per serving: 236
Fat: 6 gm. Cholesterol: 65 mg.
Sodium: 344 mg. with salt; 222 mg. without salt
For exchange diets, count: 3 lean meat,
1 bread/starch

Preparation time: 60 min.

139

MEDITERRANEAN COD
YIELD: 4 4-OZ. SERVINGS

★ ★ ★

1 medium onion, sliced
1 TB. vegetable oil
1/4 tsp. garlic powder
1 15-oz. can Italian style
    stewed tomatoes
1/4 c. salsa
1/4 tsp. cinnamon
1 lb. cod, cut into 4 portions

In a 1 1/2-qt. microwave dish, MICROWAVE onion, oil, and garlic for 3 minutes. Drain and stir in tomatoes, salsa, and cinnamon. Place cod fillets in tomato mixture. Cover and MICROWAVE on high power for 4 to 6 minutes or until fish is flaky.

Calories per 4-oz. serving: 167
Fat: 5 gm. Cholesterol: 47 mg.
Sodium: 310 mg.
For exchange diets, count: 3 lean meat

Preparation time: 15 min.

WHITE FISH CREOLE
YIELD: 4 4-OZ. SERVINGS

★ ★ ★

1 lb. Blue Hake Loins or other
   white fish fillet
2 tsp. margarine
1 c. chopped fresh tomatoes

*Creole Seasoning
(Yield = 1/3 c.):*
2 TB. paprika
1 1/2 tsp. salt (optional)
2 tsp. each black pepper, red
   pepper, and white pepper
1 tsp. thyme

Place 4 frozen fish fillets on a baking sheet and top each with 1/2
tsp. margarine. Combine ingredients for seasoning in a shaker
container. Sprinkle over fish (about 1/2 tsp. per fillet). Label
remaining seasoning and save for later use on vegetables, corn on
the cob, or meats. Bake fillets at 400° F. for 15 minutes.
Sprinkle chopped tomatoes over fillets, and bake 5 more minutes.

Calories per 4-oz. serving: 220
Fat: 8 gm. Cholesterol: 80 mg.
Sodium: 350 mg. (To reduce sodium, omit salt.)
For exchange diets, count: 4 lean meat

Preparation time: 25 min.

GRILLED PORK A LA ORANGE
YIELD: 4 3-OZ. SERVINGS

★ ★ ★

1 lb. lean pork chops, scored in
  a criss-cross pattern
1/4 c. frozen orange juice
  concentrate
1 TB. brown sugar
1/4 tsp. ground cloves
1 TB. Dijon mustard

Trim pork well. Broil or grill until nearly done (7 to 10 minutes
on each side). Combine other ingredients and pour 1/2 of the
mixture over chops. Broil or grill 2 more minutes. Turn and pour
remaining sauce on other side. Broil or grill 2 more minutes.
Serve. Garnish with an orange slice.

Calories per 3-oz. serving: 241
Fat: 9 gm. Cholesterol: 83 mg.
Sodium: 115 mg.
For exchange diets, count: 1 bread/starch,
3 lean meat

Preparation time: 30 min.

MARINATED PORK KABOBS
YIELD: 4 4-OZ. SERVINGS

★ ★ ★

1 lb. boneless lean pork
  shoulder, well trimmed
1/2 c. ketchup
2 TB. lemon juice
2 TB. brown sugar
1 tsp. reduced-sodium soy
  sauce
1 tsp. minced onion
4 small onions, halved
1 green pepper, cut into
  wedges
1 tomato cut into wedges or 8
  cherry tomatoes
1 15-oz. can whole potatoes

To prepare marinade, combine ketchup, lemon juice, brown
sugar, soy sauce, and minced onion in a bowl. Cube pork and
marinate for at least 30 minutes. Remove meat from bowl.
Thread pork cubes, onion, pepper, tomato, and potatoes onto 4
skewers. Broil or grill for 5 to 7 minutes on each side. While
kabobs are grilling, transfer leftover marinade to saucepan and
bring to a boil. Reduce heat to simmer. Pour marinade over
kabobs just before serving.

Calories per 4-oz. serving: 260
Fat: 12 gm. Cholesterol: 82 mg.
Sodium: 242 mg.
For exchange diets, count: 3 lean meat, 1 vegetable, 1 bread/starch

Preparation time: 50 min.

HAWAIIAN PORK
YIELD: 8 4-OZ. SERVINGS

★ ★ ★

2 lb. lean pork loin
1/3 c. lemon juice
2 TB. vegetable oil
2 TB. shredded onion
1/4 tsp. garlic powder
1/4 tsp. salt
1 tsp. ginger
1 1/2 tsp. curry powder
1/2 c. pineapple juice

Place well-trimmed pork loin in a shallow pan. Combine remaining ingredients and pour over loin. Marinate in the refrigerator for at least 30 minutes or up to 24 hours. Broil or grill the loin for 15 to 25 minutes on each side, placing meat 4 to 6 inches from heat element. Pork is done when an internal temperature of 170° F. is reached. Baste with marinade twice during grilling. This meat is tasty as a leftover.

Calories per 4-oz. serving: 249
Fat: 15 gm. Cholesterol: 83 mg.
Sodium: 118 mg.
For exchange diets, count: 4 lean meat, 1 fat

Preparation time: 90 min.

Speed Alert: Depending on thickness of pork loin, this recipe may take up to 90 minutes.

MEAT LOAVES ITALIANO
YIELD: 4 4-OZ. SERVINGS

★ ★ ★

1 lb. lean ground beef
1 tsp. basil
1/4 tsp. garlic powder
1/4 tsp. fennel
1/2 tsp. oregano
1/4 tsp. brown sugar
8 oz. no added salt tomato
   sauce
2 oz. mozzarella cheese,
   grated
Fresh parsley garnish

Combine meat with basil, garlic, fennel, oregano, and brown sugar in a bowl. Mix well, then shape into 4 loaves. Put on microwave meat tray and MICROWAVE for 4 minutes on high or broil in oven or on grill for 20 to 25 minutes. Drain well, then transfer to oven-safe meat platter. Pour tomato sauce over loaves, top with shredded cheese, and broil for 4 to 6 minutes. Garnish with parsley before serving. Recipe can be doubled, prepared, and frozen.

Calories per 3-oz. serving: 203
Fat: 6 gm. Cholesterol: 76 mg.
Sodium: 121 mg.
For exchange diets, count: 3 lean meat

Preparation time: 20 min.

145

Roast Pork Loin with Cumberland Sauce
Yield: 8 4-oz. servings

★ ★ ★

> 2 lb. pork loin, well trimmed
> 1 small can fruit cocktail in juice
> 1/4 c. frozen orange juice concentrate
> 1/4 c. currant jelly
> 2 TB. sherry
> 1/2 tsp. ginger
> 2 TB. cornstarch
> 2 TB. lemon juice

Grill loin 4 to 6 inches from flame on grill or broiler. Cook for 15 to 25 minutes on each side. Meanwhile, in a small saucepan, combine lemon juice and cornstarch. Drain fruit and reserve juice. Add orange juice concentrate, jelly, sherry, ginger, and reserved juice to the saucepan. Heat the mixture, stirring constantly until it thickens. Pour in fruit. Serve hot with grilled meat.

Calories per 4-oz. serving: 290
Fat: 12 gm. Cholesterol: 80 mg.
Sodium: 60 mg.
For exchange diets, count: 4 lean meat, 1 fruit

Preparation time: 40 min.

SIRLOIN BARBECUE
YIELD: 8 4-OZ. SERVINGS

★ ★ ★

2 lb. sirloin, well trimmed
1/2 tsp. salt
1/4 tsp. pepper
1 TB. vegetable oil
1/3 c. water
1 8-oz. can tomato sauce
1/2 c. chopped onion
1/2 tsp. garlic powder
2 TB. each lemon juice,
  vinegar, and
  brown sugar
1 tsp. dry mustard

Place sirloin in a shallow pan. Combine remaining ingredients and pour over meat. Cover and marinate for at least 30 minutes (or up to 24 hours) in the refrigerator. Broil or grill sirloin for 12 minutes on each side, placing meat 4 inches from heat element. Brush with marinade during last 5 minutes of cooking. This meat is tasty as a leftover.

Calories per 4-oz. serving: 229
Fat: 9 gm. Cholesterol: 72 mg.
Sodium: 374 mg. To reduce sodium, use no added salt tomato sauce.
For exchange diets, count: 4 lean meat

Preparation time: 60 min.

TORTILLA CHEESEBURGERS
YIELD: 4 4-OZ. SERVINGS

★ ★ ★

1 lb. lean ground beef
1/2 tsp. cumin
1/8 tsp. pepper
1/2 c. chopped tomato
1/2 c. chopped lettuce
1/2 c. part-skim cheddar
cheese, shredded
4 flour tortillas, warmed

Combine ground beef, cumin, and pepper, mixing lightly. Form into 4 patties. Place on a broiler pan or on the outdoor grill about 3 to 4 inches from the heat. Broil to desired doneness, turning once. Top half of each tortilla with equal portions of tomato, lettuce, and cheese. Place burger on top and fold tortilla.

Calories per filled tortilla: 299
Fat: 9 gm. Cholesterol: 66 mg.
Sodium: 337 mg.
For exchange diets, count: 4 lean meat,
1 bread/starch

Preparation time: 30 min.

WESTERN BROIL
YIELD: 4 8-OZ. SERVINGS

★ ★ ★

---

1 lb. round steak, cut 1-inch
  thick
1/2 c. light soy sauce
2 TB. honey
1 TB. lemon juice
2 scallions, finely chopped
1/4 tsp. garlic powder
3/4 c. sliced carrots, steamed
1 1/2 c. pea pods, steamed

Combine soy sauce, honey, lemon juice, scallions and garlic
powder in a small bowl. Place steak in a pie pan and pour
marinade over the steak, turning to coat. Marinate in the
refrigerator for at least 30 minutes or up to 24 hours. Discard the
marinade. Place steak on a broiler rack, so surface of meat is 3
inches from the heat. Broil for 20 minutes, turning once.
Meanwhile, arrange steamed carrots and peas around outside
edges of a serving platter. Carve beef into 4 servings and place in
the middle of platter. Serve.

Calories per 8-oz. serving: 240
Fat: 6 gm. Cholesterol: 72 mg.
Sodium: 692 mg. To reduce sodium, use 1/4 c. light soy sauce.
For exchange diets, count: 4 lean meat, 1 vegetable

Preparation time: 60 min.

COLD VEGETABLE PASTA WITH LEMON
YIELD: 8 3/4-C. SERVINGS

★ ★ ★

1 1/2 c. spiral vegetable
macaroni

1 c. frozen peas

2 large carrots, washed well
and sliced diagonally

1/3 c. chopped celery

2 TB. fresh chives or onion

4 oz. fresh mushrooms, wiped
clean and sliced

1 pkg. lemon and herb salad
dressing mix

2 TB. water

1/4 c. vinegar

1/3 c. vegetable oil

Cook macaroni according to package instructions. Put drained
macaroni in 2-quart salad bowl. Combine peas and carrots in a
covered microwave dish and MICROWAVE for 4 minutes. Drain
and add to macaroni. Stir in celery, chives, and mushrooms.
Refrigerate. Combine dressing mix with water and vinegar in a
shaker jar. Add oil and shake again. Just before serving, add 1/2
of dressing to the salad and toss. Save remaining dressing for
fresh greens.

Calories per 3/4-c. serving: 132
Fat: 4 gm. Cholesterol: 0
Sodium: 127 mg.
For exchange diets, count: 1 bread/starch,
1 vegetable, 1 fat

Preparation time: 30 min.

Note: The secret to tasty pasta salad is to keep the water boiling
during cooking, to cook only 8 to 10 minutes and to drain and
rinse with cold water immediately.

EGGPLANT AND TOMATO PARMESAN
YIELD: 4 1-C. SERVINGS

★ ★ ★

> 1 medium eggplant (or zucchini), peeled
>
> 2 medium tomatoes, chopped
>
> 6 oz. no added salt V-8 juice
>
> 1/2 c. oatmeal or bread crumbs
>
> 1 tsp. basil
>
> 1/4 tsp. oregano
>
> 1/2 tsp. garlic powder
>
> 1/2 c. or 2 oz. shredded part-skim mozzarella cheese
>
> 2 TB. Parmesan cheese

Preheat oven to 350° F. (Recipe can be microwaved.) Spray 8-inch square baking dish with nonstick cooking spray. Cut eggplant lengthwise into 1/2-inch slices. Layer into the baking dish; top with tomatoes. In small bowl, combine all other ingredients except cheeses. Spread over vegetables and cover evenly with cheeses. Bake for 35 minutes until golden brown or MICROWAVE on high power for 15 minutes.

Calories per 1-c. serving: 144
Fat: 4 gm.   Cholesterol: 10 mg.
Sodium: 118 mg.
For exchange diets, count: 2 vegetable, 1/2 bread/starch, 1 lean meat

Preparation time: 25 min.

ESCALLOPED CABBAGE
YIELD: 8 1-C. SERVINGS

★ ★ ★

3 qt. water
1 small head cabbage
2 TB. margarine
1/4 c. flour
1 c. skim milk
1 tsp. salt-free seasoning for
 vegetables,
 such as Lawrys or Parsley
 Patch
1/2 tsp. caraway seed
1 oz. mozarella cheese
1/2 tsp. salt (optional)
1/2 c. salad croutons

Preheat oven to 350° F. Bring water to a boil in 4-quart pan.
Wash cabbage and slice into bite-sized chunks. Place cabbage in
boiling water and cook for 15 minutes. Drain. Meanwhile, melt
margarine in a small skillet or saucepan and stir in flour.
Gradually add milk, and cook over medium heat until thickened.
Stir in seasoning, caraway seed, mozarella cheese, and optional
salt. Spoon cabbage into 3 qt. baking dish. Fold in sauce and top
with croutons. Bake for 20 minutes. This may be prepared and
frozen for later use.

Calories per 1-c. serving: 113
Fat: 3 gm. Cholesterol: 9 mg.
Sodium: 169 mg. with salt, 107 mg. without salt
For exchange diets, count: 1 bread/starch,
1 fat

Preparation time: 55 min.

FANCY ROASTED POTATOES
YIELD: 6 1-C. SERVINGS

★ ★ ★

1/2 c. crushed corn flakes
2 TB. margarine, melted
1/2 tsp. thyme
1/2 tsp. marjoram
1/4 tsp. pepper
1/2 tsp. salt, optional
5 large potatoes, peeled and
cut into quarters

Preheat oven to 450° F. In shallow baking pan, thoroughly blend all ingredients except potatoes. Add potatoes and turn to coat evenly with crumbs. Bake for 60 minutes or until potatoes are tender. To save time, steam the potatoes in a covered dish for 10 minutes in the MICROWAVE, then roll in crumbs and bake. This reduces the baking time to 15 minutes.

Calories per 1-c. serving: 205
Fat: 3 gm. Cholesterol: 0
Sodium: 252 mg. with salt; 129 mg. without salt
For exchange diets, count: 2 bread/starch, 1 fat

Preparation time: 30 min. if microwaved

GREEN BEAN AND DILLY STIR-FRY
YIELD: 4 1-C. SERVINGS

★ ★ ★

4 tsp. vegetable oil
1 1/2 lb. green beans, washed
  and trimmed
6 scallions, sliced
1/4 c. chopped fresh dill
3 TB. red wine vinegar
1/2 tsp. salt (optional)

Place washed and trimmed beans in a microwave dish with 2 TB. water. Cover and MICROWAVE on high power for 5 minutes. Drain. Heat oil in large skillet over high heat; add beans and stir-fry for 4 minutes, until brown specks appear on beans. Add scallions, dill, vinegar, and salt. Cook for 8 more minutes over medium heat. Serve hot.

Calories per 1-c. serving: 108
Fat: 5 gm. Cholesterol: 0
Sodium: 285 mg.with salt; 41 mg. without salt
For exchange diets, count: 2 vegetable, 1 fat

Preparation time: 20 min.

Italian Potato Salad
Yield: 4 1-c. servings

★ ★ ★

> 2 c. cooked potato chunks
> 1 c. steamed pea pods
> 1/2 c. sliced radishes
> 2 TB. chopped scallions or
>   chives
> 1/2 c. reduced-calorie Italian
>   dressing

Wash and slice potatoes into a microwave dish. Add 2 TB. water, then steam until tender (about 10 minutes on high power). Steam pea pods in same fashion in covered microwave dish for 3 minutes. Drain potatoes and pea pods rinsing with cold water. Transfer to a serving bowl. Combine with radishes and scallions or chives. Chill 15 min. Toss with dressing just before serving.

Calories per 1-c. serving: 108
Fat: 3 gm. Cholesterol: 0
Sodium: 236 mg.
For exchange diets, count: 1 bread/starch,
1 vegetable, 1/2 fat

Preparation time: 45 min.

LEMON ZUCCHINI
YIELD: 4 1-C. SERVINGS

★ ★ ★

4 small zucchini, peeled and
   sliced thin
2 TB. water
2 TB. chopped onion
1/3 c. parsley
1 TB. margarine
1/2 tsp. grated lemon peel
2 TB. lemon juice

In a covered dish, combine zucchini with water. Cover and
MICROWAVE on high power for 5 minutes. Drain. Meanwhile,
saute onion and parsley in margarine in a skillet. Stir in lemon
peel and juice. Add steamed zucchini to the pan and toss. Serve
hot.

Calories per 1-c. serving: 36
Fat: 3 gm. Cholesterol: 0
Sodium: 1 mg.
For exchange diets, count: 1 vegetable, 1/2 fat

Preparation time: 15 min.

PARTY POTATO SALAD
YIELD: 8 1/2-C. SERVINGS

★ ★ ★

3 c. cooked, diced potatoes,
    about 5 potatoes
1/2 c. frozen green peas,
    thawed
1/4 c. diced red pepper
1 TB. onion, chopped
1 hard cooked egg, diced

Dressing:
1/2 c. nonfat yogurt
1/2 c. light or reduced-calorie
    mayonnaise
1 tsp. sugar
1 TB. Dijon-style or regular
    prepared mustard
1/4 tsp. salt
1/2 tsp. pepper

Peel, dice, and steam potatoes until tender. This requires about
25 minutes on the stovetop or about 10 minutes in the
MICROWAVE (with 2 TB. water in a covered dish). Combine
potatoes with remaining salad ingredients in a 2-quart salad
bowl. Combine dressing ingredients and pour over vegetables.
Toss until well blended. Serve immediately or chill for 24 hours.

Calories per 1/2-c. serving: 132
Fat: 6 gm. Cholesterol: 42 mg.
Sodium: 193 mg.
For exchange diets, count: 1 bread/starch, 1 fat

Preparation time: 30 min.

157

Sinless Scalloped Corn
Yield: 4 3/4-c. servings

★ ★ ★

> 2 c. whole kernel corn (or 16-oz. package frozen corn)
>
> 1/8 c. chopped onion
>
> 1/4 c. skim milk
>
> 1 egg or 1/4 c. liquid egg substitute
>
> 1/4 tsp. pepper
>
> · 4 wheat crackers with unsalted tops, crushed

Preheat oven to 350° F. (Recipe can be microwaved.) If corn is frozen, defrost until the kernels are loose. Put corn into a 1-quart casserole dish sprayed with nonstick cooking spray. Add other ingredients. Stir well. MICROWAVE on high power for 20 minutes until mixture is thick or bake at 350° F. for 45 minutes. This freezes well.

Calories per 3/4-c. serving: 113
Fat: 3 gm. Cholesterol: 63 mg. with egg; 0 with sub.
Sodium: 39 mg.
For exchange diets, count: 1 1/2 bread/starch

Preparation time: 30 min.

SPAGHETTI SALAD
YIELD: 4 1-C. SERVINGS

★ ★ ★

3 oz. whole wheat spaghetti
1/3 c. no added salt tomato juice
1 1/2 tsp. dry Good Seasons
    Garlic and Herb Dressing Mix
1 tsp. oil
1 tsp. lemon juice
1 zucchini, sliced thin
1/4 c. chopped celery
4 oz. mushrooms, sliced thin

Cook spaghetti according to package directions, being careful not to overcook. Rinse with cold water, and drain well. Chop zucchini, celery, and mushrooms and put into 2-quart salad bowl. In shaker container, combine tomato juice, dressing mix, oil, and lemon juice. Transfer drained spaghetti to salad bowl, and pour dressing over spaghetti and vegetables just before serving.

Calories per 1-c. serving: 123
Fat: 2 gm. Cholesterol: 0
Sodium: 208 mg.
For exchange diets, count: 1 1/2 bread/starch

Preparation time: 20 min.

STUFFED TOMATOES
YIELD: 4 WHOLE TOMATO SERVINGS

★ ★ ★

1/2 c. orzo (rice-shaped pasta)
1/2 c. shredded farmer cheese
1/4 c. diced celery
1 tsp. dill weed
1 TB. liquid vegetable oil
1 tsp. lemon juice
1/2 tsp. salt (optional)
1/4 tsp. pepper
4 large tomatoes

Cook orzo according to package directions, taking care not to overcook. Drain and rinse under cold water. In medium mixing bowl, combine orzo with all remaining ingredients except tomatoes. Cut tops off tomatoes and scoop out the pulp and seeds. Stuff each tomato with 1/4 of the orzo mixture.

Calories per 1-tomato serving: 144
Fat: 7 gm. Cholesterol: 10 mg.
Sodium: 409 mg. with salt; 165 mg. without salt
For exchange diets, count: 1 bread/starch, 1 vegetable, 1 fat

Preparation time: 15 min.

SUMMER BAKED BEANS
YIELD: 16 1/2-c. SERVINGS

★ ★ ★

12 oz. dried navy or black beans	*Sauce:*
	16 oz. no added salt tomato sauce
1/2 c. onion, chopped	1/2 tsp. each garlic powder and basil
1 green pepper, diced	2 tsp. Worcestershire sauce
1/2 c. diced celery	2 tsp. lemon juice
12 oz. beer	3 TB. brown sugar
4 c. water	1 TB. prepared mustard
	1/8 tsp. cayenne (optional)

Soak beans 12 hours or overnight in 3-qt. saucepan with 1 qt. water. Drain. Combine beans, vegetables, beer, and 1 quart water in 3-quart saucepan and simmer for 2 1/2 hours. Drain well and transfer to 1 1/2-quart baking dish. Combine ingredients for sauce and stir into beans and vegetables. Bake at 350° F. for 15 to 20 minutes uncovered, or MICROWAVE in covered dish for 8 to 10 minutes until heated through. These beans may be fully prepared and frozen.

Calories per 1/2-c. serving: 108
Fat: 1 gm. Cholesterol: 0
Sodium: 24 mg.
For exchange diets, count: 1 bread/starch,
1/2 lean meat

Preparation time: Start day before; 3 hours day of serving.

Speed Alert: This recipe must be started the day before, and then requires 3 hours to prepare the day of serving. To save time, purchase cooked beans or use fast-soak method. This calls for covering beans with water, bringing to a boil for 15 minutes, removing from heat, and covering for 45 to 60 minutes. The fast-soak method replaces overnight soaking.

SOUTHERN VEGETABLE MEDLEY
YIELD: 4 1-C. SERVINGS

★ ★ ★

1 c. no added salt tomato juice
1 1/2 c. whole kernel corn
1 c. sliced, peeled zucchini
2 TB. brown sugar

Combine all ingredients and simmer uncovered on medium heat for 45 minutes or MICROWAVE on high power in deep covered 2-quart casserole dish for 18 minutes. Mixture will thicken.

Calories per 1-c. serving: 109
Fat: 1 gm. Cholesterol: 0
Sodium: 16 mg.
For exchange diets, count: 1 bread/starch,
1 vegetable

Preparation time: 25 min.

WILD RICE AND VEGETABLE SALAD
YIELD: 4 3/4-C. SERVINGS

★ ★ ★

1/2 c. long grain wild rice

1 c. water

Dash salt

2 TB. fresh dill or 1/2 tsp. dill
weed

2 TB. lemon juice

1 TB. vegetable oil

1/2 tsp. each grated lemon
peel and Dijon mustard

1/4 tsp. pepper

1/2 c. fresh carrot slices

1/2 c. chopped fresh broccoli

1/4 c. onion, chopped

1/2 c. fresh cauliflower, in
small pieces

Cook rice in water with salt until tender. Drain and rinse.
Combine the next 7 ingredients for dressing in a salad bowl,
using a whisk. Add vegetables and rice; toss and serve. This
keeps well for several days in the refrigerator.

Calories per 3/4-c. serving: 130
Fat: 4 gm. Cholesterol: 0
Sodium: 43 mg.
For exchange diets, count: 1 bread/starch,
1 vegetable, 1 fat

Preparation time: 40 min.

163

WILD RICE FOR PICNICS
YIELD: 4 1-C. SERVINGS

★ ★ ★

1/2 c. wild rice
2 c. water
8 oz. fresh mushrooms, sliced
1/2 c. scallions, diced
1 tsp. vegetable oil
1/2 lb. asparagus, chopped
3 med. carrots, sliced thin
2 TB. oil
1/4 c. vinegar
2 tsp. sugar
1 1/2 tsp. dry Good Seasons
    Lemon and Herb Dressing
    Mix

Heat water to boiling and add wild rice. Cook for 25 minutes, then rinse with cold water and drain well. Meanwhile, slice mushrooms, scallion, asparagus, and carrots. Place 1 tsp. oil in a 2-quart microwave-safe baking dish. Put sliced vegetables in oil, and cover. MICROWAVE on high power for 6 minutes. Uncover and stir to cool. Combine 2 TB. oil, vinegar, sugar, and dressing mix in shaker container. Place drained rice and cooled vegetables in 2-quart salad bowl and chill. Pour dressing and toss just before serving.

Calories per 1-c. serving: 208
Fat: 8 gm. Cholesterol: 0
Sodium: 217 mg.
For exchange diets, count: 1 bread/starch,
2 vegetable,1 fat

Preparation time: 35 min.

BLUEBERRY AND PINEAPPLE DESSERT CUPS
YIELD: 4 1-CUP SERVINGS

★ ★ ★

> 1 3-oz. pkg. of sugar-free
>   lemon gelatin
> 1 c. pineapple juice
> 1 1/2 c. nonfat yogurt
> 2 c. fresh blueberries

Bring pineapple juice to a boil. Pour over gelatin in 2-qt. bowl
and stir until dissolved. Chill until slightly thickened (about 1
hour). Blend in yogurt and blueberries. Pour into 4 dessert cups,
and chill firm. Garnish with pineapple chunks on a skewer.

Calories per 1-c. serving: 119
Fat: 0 Cholesterol: 0
Sodium: 60 mg.
For exchange diets, count: 1 fruit, 1/2 skim milk

Preparation time: 2 hours

Speed Alert: This recipe requires 2 hours for dessert cups to
chill firm.

CHEESECAKE WITH FRUIT SAUCE
YIELD: 8 SLICES

★ ★ ★

> 1 Royal Lite Cheesecake mix
> 2 c. chopped rhubarb,
>   strawberries, cherries,
>   peaches, or mixture of your
>   favorite fruit
> 1 pkg. sugar-free raspberry
>   gelatin

Prepare cheesecake according to package directions and refrigerate. Bring 1/4 c. water to a boil in a medium saucepan. Add rhubarb. Cover and simmer for 15 minutes. Stir in gelatin. Chill and serve as a sauce for the cheesecake.

Calories per 1/8 pie: 128
Fat: 7 gm.   Cholesterol: 20 mg.
Sodium: 310
For exchange diets, count: 1 skim milk, 1 fat

FROZEN CHOCOLATE CHEATCAKE
YIELD: 8 SLICES

★ ★ ★

8 oz. light (look for 50% fat)
   cream cheese, softened

1/3 c. sugar

2 tsp. vanilla

3 TB. cocoa

3 egg whites

2 TB. sugar

1 c. nonfat cottage cheese,
   blended smooth

Combine cheese, 1/3 c. sugar, and vanilla. Beat egg whites until frothy and gradually add sugar until stiff peaks form. Fold blended cottage cheese and egg whites into the cheese and sugar mixture. Pour mixture into a souffle pan sprayed with nonstick cooking spray. Freeze for 1 1/2 hours. Thaw for 10 minutes and serve.

Calories per 1/8 pie: 128
Fat: 6 gm.   Cholesterol: 20 mg.
Sodium: 310 mg.
For exchange diets, count: 1 skim milk, 1 fat

Preparation time: 2 hr.

Speed Alert: This recipe requires 2 hours.

FROZEN GRASSHOPPER DESSERT
YIELD: 8 SLICES

★ ★ ★

1/4 c. skim milk
30 large marshmallows
2 TB. creme de menthe
2 egg whites
2 TB. sugar
1 c. nonfat yogurt

Combine milk and marshmallows in enamel or no-stick pan. Cook over medium heat until marshmallows are melted or MICROWAVE the mixture in a mixing bowl for 2 1/2 minutes. Stir until smooth. Cool 2 minutes, then stir in liqueur. Chill 10 minutes in the refrigerator. Meanwhile, whip egg whites until frothy and gradually add sugar until mixture is stiff. Fold yogurt and whites into the marshmallow mixture, and pour into an 8 inch square pan. Freeze 1 1/2 hours, covered. Remove from freezer 15 minutes before serving to soften. Cut into 8 squares.

Calories per slice: 165
Fat: less than 1 gm. Cholesterol: 1 mg.
Sodium: 41 mg.
For exchanges diets, count: 2 Bread/Starch

Preparation time: 2 hr.

Speed Alert: This recipe requires 2 hours to freeze firm.

HONEYDEW WHIP
YIELD: 8 SERVINGS

★ ★ ★

1 lg. honeydew melon
1/4 c. each lemon juice and
    lime juice
1 c. water
2/3 c.+ 2 TB. sugar
5 envelopes unflavored
    gelatin
2 TB. orange or peach liqueur
2 egg whites

In blender, puree small amounts of melon, lemon, and lime juice
and pour into large bowl. Combine water, 2/3 c. sugar, and
gelatin in a small mixing bowl and let stand for 4 minutes.
MICROWAVE this gelatin mixture at full power uncovered for 3
minutes or just to boiling and stir to dissolve the sugar and
gelatin. Add to melon, then briskly stir in liqueur and chill for 30
minutes. Mixture should mound when spooned. Beat egg whites
with 2 TB. of sugar until soft peaks form. Fold whites into chilled
melon mixture and transfer to a souffle dish. Refrigerate for 4
hours or place in freezer for 1 1/2 hours and then transfer to
refrigerator for 30 minutes. Slice and serve.

Calories per 1/8th of recipe: 156
Fat: 0   Cholesterol: 0
Sodium: 13 mg.
For exchange diets, count: 1 bread/starch, 1 fruit

Preparation time: 10 min. Refrigerate 4 hours.

Speed Alert: This recipe requires a minimum of 2 hours
preparation time.

LEMON STRAWBERRY SUPREME
YIELD: 8 SLICES

★ ★ ★

2 pt. strawberries
1/2 c. skim milk
1 envelope unflavored gelatin
1/2 c. sugar
2 TB. grated fresh lemon peel
1/4 c. lemon juice
1 1/2 c. nonfat yogurt

Clean strawberries and chill. In 1-quart saucepan, combine milk and gelatin. Set aside for 5 minutes, then stir in sugar. Stir over low heat until gelatin and sugar are dissolved. Stir in peel and juice. Cool to room temperature, then chill until syrupy, about 15 minutes. Meanwhile, spray a quiche or vegetable dish (with 2-inch deep sides) with nonstick cooking spray. Fold yogurt into gelatin mixture and spoon into quiche dish. Cut the strawberries in half and place on top of lemon mixture. Chill at least 1 1/2 hours, slice and serve.

Calories per slice (1/8 pie): 101
Fat: 1 gm. Cholesterol: 2 mg.
Sodium: 84 mg.
For exchange diets, count: 2 fruit

Preparation time: 15 minutes. Refrigerate 2 hours.

Speed Alert: This recipe requires 2 hours.

MILE HIGH PEACH PIE
YIELD: 8 SLICES

★ ★ ★

16 2 x 2-inch graham crackers
2 TB. margarine
4 fresh peaches
1 c. sugar
2 egg whites
1 tsp. vanilla
1 tsp. lemon juice
1 c. whipped topping
Pinch salt

Crush crackers in a blender or with a rolling pin and transfer to a pie plate. Melt margarine and stir into cracker crumbs, pressing mixture evenly over bottom and up sides of the pan. Peel the peaches, chop fine, and set aside. In a medium mixing bowl, combine sugar, egg whites, vanilla, and lemon juice, and beat at medium speed for 15 minutes or until mixture is stiff. Fold in whipped topping and peaches. Pile lightly into prepared crumb shell. Chill for 1 1/2 hours and serve.

Calories per 1/8 pie: 210
Fat: 5 gm. Cholesterol: 0
Sodium: 113 mg.
For exchange diets, count: 1 bread, 1 fat,
1 1/2 fruit

Preparation time: 30 min. Refrigerate 1 1/2 hr.

Speed Alert: This recipe requires 2 hours.

OAT BRAN CRUNCHIES
YIELD: 30 COOKIES

★ ★ ★

1/2 c. margarine	1/4 tsp. salt
1/2 c. brown sugar	3/4 c. oatmeal
1 TB. water	3/4 c. oatflake cereal, lightly crushed (such as Honey Bunches of Oats or Clusters)
1 tsp. vanilla	
1 egg or 1/4 c. liquid egg substitute	
1/2 c. flour	1/4 c. oat bran
1/4 c. whole wheat flour	2 TB. sugar
1/2 tsp. baking soda	1 tsp. cinnamon

Preheat oven to 350 F. Cream margarine and sugar with electric mixer until well blended. Add water, vanilla, and egg, beating well. Combine flours, soda, and salt and add to creamed mixture. Add oatmeal, oat flake cereal, and oat bran. Drop dough by spoonfuls onto a no-stick baking sheet. Combine 2 TB. sugar and 1 tsp. cinnamon in a small bowl. Dip flat bottom of a glass into the sugar and cinnamon mixture and use to press dough flat. Bake for 7 minutes until browned. Cool on a wire rack. Store in covered container when cooled.

Calories per cookie: 80
Fat: 4 gm. Cholesterol: 9 mg. with egg; 0 with substitute
Sodium: 70 mg.
For exchange diets, count: 1/2 bread/starch,
1 fat

Preparation time: 30 min.

PEACH AMBROSIA
YIELD: 4 1-CUP SERVINGS

★ ★ ★

1/4 c. cold water
1 envelope unflavored gelatin
1/2 c. skim milk
2 envelopes ALBA 77 Vanilla
  Shake
1 tsp. vanilla
6 large ice cubes
2 medium peaches, peeled
  and chopped
1/3 c. coconut

In a small saucepan, sprinkle gelatin over water and let stand for
1 minute. Stir over low heat until gelatin is dissolved. In blender
container, combine milk, ALBA 77, vanilla, and gelatin
mixture. Cover and process for 30 seconds on low speed, adding
ice cubes one at a time. Process at high speed until mixture
thickens. Transfer to a bowl and fold in peaches. Spoon into 4
dessert dishes and sprinkle with coconut. Chill for 1 hour and
serve.

Calories per serving: 104
Fat: 2 gm. Cholesterol: 4 mg.
Sodium: 36 mg.
For exchange diets, count: 1 skim milk,
1/2 fruit

Preparation time: 20 min. Refrigerate 1 hr.

Speed Alert: This recipe requires over 1 hour from start to
finish.

PEACHES AND CHEESE PIE
YIELD: 8 SLICES

★ ★ ★

---

1 Royal Lite Cheese Cake Mix
2 TB. margarine
1 1/2 c. skim milk
2 ripe firm peaches, peeled
and diced

Combine graham crackers from the cheese cake mix with 2 TB. melted margarine. Press into an 8-inch pie plate. Refrigerate. Pour 1 1/2 c. skim milk into small mixing bowl. Add cheese cake mix and beat at low speed until blended. Beat at medium speed 3 more minutes. Meanwhile, wash, peel, and dice peaches. Fold peaches into the cheese cake mixture, then pour into prepared crust. Chill for 1 hour. Slice and serve.

Calories per 1/8th pie: 60
Fat: 2 gm. Cholesterol: 2 mg.
Sodium: 93 mg.
For exchange diets, count: 1 skim milk,
1/2 fat

Preparation time: 20 min. Refrigerate 1 hr.

PEACH MELBA MERINGUE PIE
YIELD: 8 SLICES

★ ★ ★

4 egg whites
1/2 c. sugar
1/4 tsp. baking powder
1/2 c. shredded coconut
1 pkg. unflavored gelatin
1/4 c. orange juice
1 1/2 c. low fat cottage cheese
1 c. plain nonfat yogurt
4 pkg. Equal® sugar
  substitute
1 1/2 c. fresh or frozen sliced
  peaches
1/4 c. reduced-calorie
  raspberry preserves

Preheat oven to 325° F. Beat egg whites stiff and gradually beat in sugar. Mix coconut with baking powder and fold into whites. Pour this into a 9-inch pie pan sprayed with nonstick cooking spray. Bake for 30 minutes. Remove from oven and cool. Soften gelatin in orange juice in saucepan, then heat until gelatin is all dissolved. Meanwhile, in a mixing bowl, beat the cottage cheese smooth with an electric mixer. Fold in yogurt, Equal®, and almond extract. Fold gelatin and peaches into cottage cheese mixture. Pour into meringue crust and chill 1 to 2 hours. Top with raspberry preserves just before serving. This pie does not keep longer than 1 day.

Calories per slice: 153
Fat: 2 gm. Cholesterol: 2 mg.
Sodium: 66 mg.
For exchange diets, count: 1 bread/starch, 1 fruit

Preparation time: 45 min. Refrigerate 2 hr.

PINEAPPLE IN POPPY SEED DRESSING
YIELD: 4 1-C. SERVINGS

★ ★ ★

1 fresh pineapple
1/2 c. pineapple juice
1 TB. lime juice
2 TB. honey
1 TB. poppy seed
1 tsp. grated lime peel

Cut pineapple in half lengthwise through crown. Remove fruit with a curved knife, leaving shells intact. Cut pineapple into chunks. Combine remaining ingredients in a shaker container. Spoon dressing over fruit and mix. Transfer to pineapple shell and serve.

Calories per 1-c. serving: 117
Fat: 1 gm. Cholesterol: 0
Sodium: 2 mg.
For exchange diets, count: 2 fruit

Preparation time: 15 min.

RHUBARB CRUNCH

YIELD: 8 1-C. SREVINGS

★ ★ ★

6 c. chopped rhubarb
1 pkg. regular or sugar-free
    raspberry gelatin
1/2 c. orange juice
2 tsp. vanilla
2/3 c. flour
1/3 c. oatmeal
1/2 c. brown sugar
1 tsp. cinnamon
1/4 c. margarine

Preheat oven to 350° F. Combine rhubarb, gelatin, vanilla, and orange juice in a 9-inch square baking dish. Use a pastry blender in a small mixing bowl to combine all remaining ingredients until they are crumbly. Sprinkle crumbs over the rhubarb. Bake for 45 minutes uncovered, just until bubbly. Cool and serve. Use vanilla nonfat yogurt, vanilla ice milk, or vanilla frozen yogurt as a topping.

Calories per 1-c. serving 178
Fat: 7 gm.   Cholesterol: 0
Sodium: 117 mg.
For exchange diets, count: 1 bread/starch, 1 fruit, 1 fat

Preparation time: 60 min.

RHUBARB STRAWBERRY CRISP
YIELD: 8 1/2-C. SERVINGS

★ ★ ★

2 1/2 c. strawberries
1 1/2 c. chopped rhubarb
1 TB. cornstarch
1/4 c. sugar

Topping:
1/2 c. oatmeal
1/2 c. flour
1/3 c. brown sugar
1/4 c. margarine
1/2 tsp. cinnamon

Preheat oven to 350° F. (Recipe can be microwaved.) Spray a 2-quart baking dish with nonstick cooking spray. Combine fruits with cornstarch and sugar in the baking dish. Use a pastry blender to mix the topping ingredients until crumbly. Sprinkle topping over fruit. MICROWAVE for 15 minutes on high power or bake for 40 minutes.

Calories per 1/2-c. serving: 155
Fat: 7 gm. Cholesterol: 0
Sodium: 73 mg.
For exchange diets, count: 1 fruit, 1 fat ,
1/2 bread/starch

Preparation time: 30 min. if microwaved, 55 min. if baked

SPRING PARFAIT
YIELD: 4 1-C. SERVINGS

★ ★ ★

10-oz. pkg. frozen raspberries,
  thawed
2 TB. lemon juice
1 c. nonfat plain yogurt
2 egg whites
1/4 c. sugar

In blender container, puree berries and lemon juice until smooth.
Strain out seeds and set in freezer. Meanwhile, beat egg whites
until frothy, then gradually add sugar until stiff peaks form. Fold
yogurt into egg white mixure. Divide egg white and yogurt
mixture into 4 dessert glasses or dishes. Spoon chilled berries on
top. Use a knife to marbelize. Freeze at least 30 minutes.
Remove from freezer 5 minutes before serving.

Calories per 1-c. serving: 140
Fat: 0 Cholesterol: 0
Sodium: 40 mg.
For exchange diets, count: 1 bread/starch,
1 fruit

Preparation time: 50 min.

STAND UP FOR STRAWBERRY PIE
YIELD: 8 SLICES

★ ★ ★

Crust:
1 1/2 c. crushed cornflakes
2 TB. margarine, melted
1 TB. sugar

Filling:
4 c. sliced strawberries
2/3 c. sugar
1 c. water
3 TB. each cornstarch and
    corn syrup
3 TB. strawberry gelatin
    (may use sugar-free)

Topping:
8 oz. vanilla low-fat yogurt

Preheat oven to 375° F. Combine ingredients for crust in a 9-inch pie plate. Press into pan and bake for 10 minutes until browned. Cool. Put sliced berries into the crust. Combine sugar, water, cornstarch, and corn syrup in a saucepan and boil for 2 minutes, stirring constantly. Remove from heat and stir in gelatin. Pour over berries. Chill for 1 1/2 hours. Top with vanilla yogurt before serving.

Calories per serving: 194
Fat: 4 gm. Cholesterol: 2 mg.
Sodium: 94 mg.
For exchange diets, count: 2 fruit, 1/2 bread/starch, 1 fat

Preparation time: 30 min.

Speed Alert: Two hours preparation time required.

STRAWBERRY ALASKA
YIELD: 12 SERVINGS

★ ★ ★

1 angel food cake mix,
   prepared according to
   package directions
4 c. low-fat frozen strawberry
   yogurt
3 egg whites
1/3 c. sugar
Pinch salt
Pinch cream of tartar

Prepare and bake cake according to package directions. Cool
completely. Let frozen yogurt soften slightly. Frost cake with
yogurt, cover with plastic wrap, and freeze immediately for 20
min. In mixing bowl, beat egg whites until foamy. Add cream of
tartar and salt. Gradually add sugar, beating constantly, until
stiff. Preheat broiler. Frost cake with meringue. Place cake 3
inches from heat source, and broil for 1 to 2 minutes, until
browned. Serve immediately. Leftover dessert may be frozen for
use later.

Calories per serving: 221
Fat: 2 gm. Cholesterol: 6 mg.
Sodium: 204 mg.
For exchange diets, count: 2 bread/starch,
1 fruit

Preparation time: 2 hr.

Speed Alert: 2 hours

STRAWBERRIES 'N CREME
YIELD: 4 3/4-CUP SERVINGS

★ ★ ★

3 c. strawberries, halved
2 TB. grenadine
2 tsp. rum extract
1/4 c. light sour cream
1 c. nonfat yogurt
1/4 c. sugar
1/4 tsp. ground nutmeg

Toss strawberries with grenadine and rum extract. Chill for 15 min. Before serving, combine light sour cream, yogurt, and sugar in a bowl. Spoon berries into individual dessert glasses, top with yogurt mixture and sprinkle with nutmeg.

Calories per 3/4-c. serving: 169
Fat: 1 gm. Cholesterol: 2 mg.
Sodium: 47 mg.
For exchange diets, count: 2 fruit, 1/2 skim milk

Preparation time: 25 min.

TORTONI CAFETTA
YIELD: 8 1/2-CUP SERVINGS

★ ★ ★

2 egg whites, beaten stiff
1 TB. instant coffee
1/8 tsp. salt
6 TB. sugar
1 c. low-fat cottage cheese,
  blended smooth
2 tsp. vanilla
1/2 tsp. almond extract

Beat egg whites and coffee until stiff. Beat in sugar slowly. Stir in flavoring. Fold blended cottage cheese into egg whites. Freeze for 45 minutes in individual serving dishes. Garnish with almonds. Remove from freezer 10 minutes before serving.

Calories per 1/2-c. serving: 59
Fat: 1 gm. Cholesterol: 1 mg.
Sodium: 150 mg.
For exchange diets, count: 1 bread/starch

Preparation time: 60 min.

Zucchini Brownies
Yield: 30 2-inch square cookies

★ ★ ★

3 c. peeled and grated
    zucchini

1 1/2 c. sugar

2/3 c. oil

3 c. flour

1/2 tsp. salt

2 tsp. soda

1/3 c. cocoa

3 tsp. vanilla

1/3 c. coconut

1/2 c. chopped almonds

Preheat oven to 350° F. Mix all ingredients together in 2-qt. mixing bowl. Spray an 8 x 15-inch pan with nonstick cooking spray. Spread batter in pan. Bake for 25 minutes or until toothpick inserted in center comes out clean. Dust with powdered sugar when cooled.

Calories per serving: 137
Fat: 6 gm. Cholesterol: 0
Sodium: 92 mg.
For exchange diets, count: 1 bread/starch, 1 fat

Preparation time: 45 min.

Nutrition Alert: This recipe contains a significant amount of sugar, and may not be a good choice for insulin-dependent diabetics. Check with your dietitian if you have questions.

FALL & WINTER

MENUS & RECIPES

A Month of Low-Fat Dinner Menus for Fall and Winter

The following dinner menus feature common foods and selected recipes from this book (noted with*). Use the dinner menus together with breakfast and lunch menus on page** to create a 40-gm. fat (or 1500-calorie) diet plan.

WEEK ONE	WEEK TWO	WEEK THREE	WEEK FOUR
1 serving *Pizza Rounds 1 c. Fresh Greens with 2 TB. No-Oil Dressing 1/2 c. Frozen Peaches 1 c. Skim Milk	1 serv. *Turkey Kabobs 1 Dinner Roll with 1 tsp. Margarine 1 sl. Angel Food Cake with 1 c. Strawberries 1 c. Skim Milk	1 serv. *Chicken Cacciatore 1 Toasted Onion Bagel with 1 tsp. Margarine 1/2 c. Blueberries 1 c. Skim Milk	3 oz. Broiled Hamburger on a Wheat Bun with Lettuce, Onion and Tomato 1/2 c. Whole Kernel Corn
1 serving *California Blend Cream Soup 2 lg. Breadsticks 2 oz. Part-skim Cheese 1 Kiwi Fruit Marinated in Gingerale 1 c. Skim Milk	1 serv. *Taco Casserole 1 c. Chopped Lettuce & Tomatoes 1/2 c. Sugar-Free Vanilla Pudding with Raisins 1 c. Skim Milk	1 serv. *Turkey Salad A La Orange 4 Wheat Crackers 1/2 c. Cranberry Juice 1 c. Skim Milk	1 serv. *Perfect Raspberry Chiffon 1 c. Skim Milk 1 serv. *Traditional Pot Roast 1 sl. White Bread from Frozen Dough with 1 tsp. Margarine
1 serv. *Almond Chicken with Vegetables Fresh Carrot Sticks 15 Fresh Green Grapes 1 c. Skim Milk	1 serv. *Steamed Fish Fillets 1 Baked Potato with 1 tsp. Margarine 1/2 c. Steamed Broccoli 1/2 c. Cherries 1 c. Skim Milk	1 serv. *Michigan Bean Soup 1 sl. Wheat Toast and 1 tsp. Margarine 1 c. Melon Balls with 1/2 c. Lime Sherbet on top 1 c. Skim Milk	1/2 c. Applesauce over 1/2 c. Ice Milk 1 c. Skim Milk 1 serv. *Turkey & Mushroom Tetrazzini
1 serv. *Harvest Casserole 1 sl. Wheat Toast 1 c. Fresh Cucumber Slices 1/2 Frozen Banana 1 c. Skim Milk	1/2 c. Chilled No Added Salt Tomato Juice 1 serv. *Pineaple Chicken 1/2 c. Quick Rice 4 Carrot Sticks 15 Red Grapes 1 c. Skim Milk	1 serv. *Fish & Potato Bake 1/2 c. Stewed Tomatoes 1/2 c. Mixed Fruit with 1 c. Nonfat Vanilla Yogurt on top	1 sl. Broiled Garlic Toast 1 Fresh Orange 1 c. Skim Milk 1 serv. *Baked Potato Burrito 1 c. Chopped Lettuce and Tomato
1 serv. *Pumpkin Soup 1 Toasted Bagel with 2 oz. Lean Ham 1 c. Fresh Greens with 1 TB. No-Oil Dressing 1/2 c. Sorbet 1 c. Skim Milk	1 serv. *Tex- mex Porkloaf 1/2 c. Squash 1 Kaiser Roll with 1/2 tsp. Margarine 1 Granny Smith Apple 1 c. Skim Milk	3 oz. Grilled Chicken Breast 1 serv. *Rice Creole 1 sl. French Bread with Margarine 1 Nectarine 1 c. Skim Milk	1/2 c. Fruit Cocktail with Sliced Bananas 1 c. Skim Milk 1 serv. *Chinese Pork and Broccoli 1/2 c. Quick Rice 1 Fresh Pear 1 c. Skim Milk
1 serv.*Chicken Stroganoff 1 Whole Wheat Roll with 1 tsp. Margarine 1 c. Shredded Cabbage with Red.-Cal. Drsg. 1/2 c. Pineapple Slices 1 c. Skim Milk	1 serv. *Tuna & Noodle Casserole Radishes and Cherry Tomatoes 1 sl. Wheat Toast 1/2 c. Orange Slices Marinated in Wine Cooler 1 c. Skim Milk	1 serv. *Shopper's Chili 6 Soda Crackers 4 Radishes 1/2 c. Apple and Pineapple Chunks 1 c. Skim Milk 3 oz. Grilled Halibut Steaks 1 Baked Potato with 1 tsp. Margarine	1 serv. *Chicken Breast Midwest 1 Wheat Roll with 1 tsp. Margarine 1/2 c. Fresh Pineapple over 1/2 c. Lime Sherbet 1 c. Skim Milk
1 serv. *Vegetable Enchiladas 1 c. Chopped Lettuce 4 Cherry Tomatoes 1/2 c. Frozen Yogurt 1 c. Skim Milk	1 serv. *London Broil 1 serv. *Baked Potato Chips 1 sl. French Bread and 1 tsp. Margarine 1/2 c. Peach and Banana Slices 1 c. Skim Milk	1 c. Fresh Veggies and 1 TB. Red.-Cal. Drsg. 1 serv. *Anita's Pretty Fruit Cups 1 c. Skim Milk	1 serv. *Fettucini Low-Fat Alfredo 1 c. Fresh Greens with 1 TB. Reduced-Calorie Italian Dressing 1/2 c. Frozen Yogurt 1 c. Skim Milk

187

A Week of Breakfast and Lunch Menus for Fall and Winter

	Breakfast	Lunch	Snacks
Monday	3/4 c. Cream of Wheat with 1/2 Banana 1 sl. French Bread toasted with 1 tsp. Margarine 1/2 c. Skim Milk	1/2 c. Tuna with 1 tsp. Mayo on a Warm Bun 1 c. Steamed California Blend Veggies 1 Granny Smith Apple 1/2 c. Skim Milk	5 Melba Rounds 1/2 c. Pineapple Juice
Tuesday	1 English Muffin Toasted with 2 Tsp. Margarine 1/2 c. Orange Juice 1/2 c. Skim Milk	2 sm. Soft Shell Tacos with 2 oz. Seasoned Ground Turkey 1 c. Chopped Lettuce & Tomato 1 Fresh Pear 1/2 c. Skim Milk	3 c. Air Popcorn 1 Apple
Wednesday	1/2 c. Oatmeal with 2 TB. Raisins 1 sl. Wheat Toast & 1 tsp. Margarine 1/2 c. Skim Milk	1 c. Chicken Noodle Soup 2 oz. Farmers Cheese 1 sl. Wheat Toast 1 Large Apple 1/2 c. Skim Milk	1 oz. Pretzels 1 Oranges
Thursday	1 Whole Bagel Toasted with 2 tsp. Peanut Butter 1/2 c. Grapefruit Juice 1/2 c. Skim Milk	1 Large Baked Potato topped with 1/2 c. Browned Ground Beef and 1/4 c. Tomato Sauce and 1/2 c. Strawberries 1/2 c. Vanilla Yogurt on top	4 sq. Graham Crackers 1/2 c. Apple Juice
Friday	2 sm. Pancake with 1/2 c. Applesauce and Cinnamon on top 1/2 c. Skim Milk	2 oz. Lean Ham with 1 c. Fresh Veggies stuffed into 1 Lg. Pita Bread 1 c. Vegetable Soup 1 /2 Grapefruit 1/2 c. Skim Milk	1/2 c. Blueberries & 1 Molasses Cookie
Saturday	1/2 c. Maltomeal 1 Bran Muffin 1/2 c. Pineapple Juice 1/2 c. Skim Milk	1 c. Tomato Soup 4 Wheat Crackers 1/2 c. Low Fat Cottage Cheese 1/2 c. Mixed Fruit 1/2 c. Skim Milk	1/4 c. Sherbet with 1 Kiwi fruit
Sunday	1/2 c. Bran Cereal 1 sl. Raisin Toast & 1 tsp. Margarine 1/2 c. Pineapple Chunks 1/2 c. Skim Milk	2 oz. Grilled Breast of Chicken on a Bun with Mustard 1 c. Steamed Green Beans with 1 tsp. Margarine 12 Grapes 1/2 c. Skim Milk	7 Animal Crackers 2 Plums

Use this week of breakfast and lunch menus together with the dinner
menus suggestions on page ** to create a 40-gm. fat (or 1500-calorie) diet plan.

Special Occasion Menus
For Fall and Winter

Tailgate Party
*Party Meal in a Bowl with
Assorted Fresh Vegetables
*Pizza Loaf
*Tailgate Salad
Fresh Cortland Apples
(stick one in your pocket for the game)

Halloween
*Mexican Corn Main Dish
*Herbed Corn Bread
*Halloween Salad
Orange Sherbet

Oktoberfest
*Rouladen
*German Potato Salad
*German Red Cabbage
Dark Rye Bread with Margarine
*Fresh Fruit Soup

Thanksgiving Dinner
*Tarragon Turkey
*Fruit Stuffing
*Cranberry Salad
*Nutty Glazed Carrots
*Cranapple Bread
*Marinated Fruit on a Platter

*Recipe is in this book. Check the index for page numbers.

Thanksgiving Brunch
*Dilly Cocktail
*Turkey Crepes
*Cold Sweet and Sour Vegetables
*Date Nut Bread
*Rolled Pumpkin Cheesecake

Holiday Cocktail Party
*Wrapped Carrots
*Nutty Mushrooms
*Popeye's Spinach Croquettes
*Chili Dip with Potato Skins
*Christmas Tree Canapes

Christmas Eve
*Christmas Bisque
*Decorated Breadsticks
*Crunchy Broccoli Salad
*Lemon Citron Crisps

Christmas Day
*Marinated Loin of Pork
.*Christmas Stuffing
*Baked Carrots and Sprouts
*Tangy Cabbage and Dried Fruit Salad
*Pumpkin Tofu Pie

New Year's Eve
*Jambalya
*Sweet and Sour Cucumbers
Wheat Rolls with Margarine
Vanilla Ice Milk with Creme de Menthe on top

*Recipe is in this book. Check index for page numbers.

New Year's Day
*Tortilla Chicken Brunch
Chopped Lettuce & Tomato on the Side
*Fruit Crunch for Sherbet

Sledding Party Potluck
*Cock-a-Leekie Soup
*Chunky Beef Chili
*Carrot Muffins
*Cathy's Cheese Pepper Bread
(Ask your friends to bring a vegetable tray)
Chocolate Frozen Yogurt Cones

Valentine's Day
*Romantic Chicken Marsala
*Green Beans with Garlic Dressing
*Fabulous French Bread
*Fruit Plate with Strawberry Dip

St. Patrick's Day
*Irish Potato Soup
*Spinach and Bacon Crunch
Fresh Greens with
*Creamy Garlic Dressing
*Lime Cheesecake

Winter Dinner Party
*Tomato Pockets
*Stuffed Sole
*Broccoli Rice Casserole
*Autumn Buns
*Pear Melba

*Recipe is in this book. Check index for the page numbers.

Bridge Club Desserts
*Chocolate Mousse
*Poppy Seed Bread
*Kiwi for Company
*Sharon B's Whole Wheat Apple Cake
*Oatbran Apple Crisp

*Recipe is in this book. Check index for page numbers.

CHILI DIP WITH POTATO SKINS
*YIELD: 8 3/4-C. SERVINGS OF DIP
AND 1/2 POTATO*

★ ★ ★

16-oz. can no added salt chili
beans
1 c. plain yogurt
1 avocado, peeled and mashed
1/2 c. scallions, chopped
5-oz. can green chilis, chopped
1/2 c. diced fresh tomato
4 oz. shredded part-skim
American cheese

Potato Skins:
4 potatoes
2 TB. margarine, melted
1 tsp. chili powder

Preheat oven to 400° F. Scrub potatoes and microwave for 6
minutes turning after 3 minutes, or bake at 400° F. for 1 hour.
Meanwhile, prepare dip: In blender container, combine beans,
yogurt, and avocado. Process until smooth. Spread over 9-inch
round flat plate. Top with scallions, chilis, tomato, and cheese.
Refrigerate. When potatoes are done, cut in half lengthwise and
scoop out pulp. Cut skins lengthwise with sharp scissors, about
1-inch wide. Arrange skins on baking sheet, brush with melted
margarine and chili powder. Bake at 475° F. for 8 to10 minutes.
Serve hot with dip.

Calories per serving: 204
Fat: 5 gm. Cholesterol: 9 mg.
Sodium: 368 mg.
For exchange diets, count: 1 1/2 bread/starch, 1 vegetable, 1 meat

Preparation time: 40 min.

CHRISTMAS TREE CANAPES
YIELD: 8 SERVINGS

★ ★ ★

> 3 oz. reduced-calorie cream
>   cheese
> 2 TB. catsup
> 1 TB. horseradish
> 1/4 tsp. garlic powder
> 1 dash cayenne
> 1/4 c. chopped fresh parsley
> 6 oz. imitation crab, thawed
>   and flaked
> 8 slices white bread

Using a Christmas tree cookie cutter, cut a Christmas tree shape
out of each slice of bread. Reserve shapes and discard edges.
Mix all ingredients into softened reduced-calorie cream cheese.
Spread this mixture evenly over slices of bread. Place under
preheated broiler until lightly browned. Serve immediately.

Calories per slice: 116
Fat: 3 gm. Cholesterol: 14 mg.
Sodium: 365 mg. To reduce sodium, use low-salt catsup.
For exchange diets, count: 1 bread/starch, 1/2 lean meat

Preparation time: 15 min.

DECORATED BREADSTICKS
YIELD: 8 SERVINGS

★ ★ ★

1 tube of soft breadstick dough
2 TB. chopped pimiento
2 TB. chopped green pepper

Preheat oven to 350° F. Unroll dough and separate into 8 strips. Twist each strip and place on an ungreased cookie sheet. Press edges down firmly. Carefully sprinkle strips on all sides with pimiento and green pepper. Bake for 15 to 18 minutes until golden brown.

Calories per breadstick: 103
Fat: 2 gm. Cholesterol: less than 5 mg.
Sodium: 230 mg.
For exchange diets, count: 1 bread/starch,
1/2 fat

Preparation time: 20 min.

DILLY COCKTAIL
YIELD: 4 3/4-C. SERVINGS

★ ★ ★

> 24 oz. no added salt vegetable
>   juice
> 1/2 tsp. dill weed
> 4 lemon slices

Cut and twist lemon slices and secure to edge of wine glass. Pour juice into goblet and sprinkle with dill weed.

Calories per 3/4-c. serving: 37
Fat: 0   Cholesterol: 0
Sodium: 47 mg.
For exchange diets, count: 1 vegetable

Preparation time: 5 min.

HOT CHOCOLATE MIX
YIELD: 4 SERVINGS

★ ★ ★

1 1/3 c. nonfat dry milk
1/4 c. cocoa
4 packets Equal® sugar
   substitute
1 qt. boiling water
1 tsp. vanilla

Mix nonfat dry milk with cocoa and Equal® in a 1 1/2 quart heat-proof container. Add the boiling water and stir to mix. Stir in vanilla and serve.

Calories per 8-oz. serving: 100
Fat: 2 gm. Cholesterol: 7 mg.
Sodium: 35 mg.
For exchange diets, count: 1 skim milk

Preparation time: 5 min.

NUTTY MUSHROOMS
YIELD: 4 SERVINGS, 5 MUSHROOMS EACH

★ ★ ★

20 fresh mushrooms
2 TB. margarine
1/4 c. chopped onion
1/4 tsp. garlic powder
1/4 c. Grape Nuts® cereal
1 TB. chopped parsley
1/4 tsp. pepper

Preheat oven to 350° F. Remove stems from mushrooms. Chop stems and set aside. Melt margarine in a skillet. Mix in chopped mushroom stems, and onions, sauteing until onions are tender. Stir in garlic powder, cereal, parsley, and pepper. Fill mushroom caps. Bake for 20 minutes and serve hot.

Calories per 5 mushrooms: 44
Fat: 3 gm. Cholesterol: 0
Sodium: 60 mg.
For exchange diets, count: 1 vegetable, 1/2 fat

Preparation time: 35 min.

PARTY MEAL IN A BOWL
YIELD: 8 SERVINGS

★ ★ ★

1 lb. round loaf crusty bread,
  such as rye, or Italian

2 10-oz. pkgs. chopped, frozen
  spinach, thawed and
  squeezed dry

8-oz. pkg. light cream cheese

3 TB. skim milk

1 TB. lemon juice

1/2 c. chopped pimiento

1/2 c. red onion, chopped

4 strips bacon, cooked,
  drained, and crumbled

1/2 tsp. white pepper

For best results, allow loaf of bread to dry out 24 hours in the open air. Remove 1 1/2-inch layer from top of loaf and chop into 1-inch cubes. Scoop out the remaining bread from the loaf and cube. Combine spinach and all remaining ingredients in a mixing bowl and chill for 30 minutes. Serve the dip in the bread bowl and use the cubes of bread as dippers.

Calories per serving: 249
Fat: 10 gm. Cholesterol: 24 mg.
Sodium: 479 mg.
For exchange diets, count: 1 1/2 bread/starch, 2 vegetable, 2 fat

Preparation time: 45 min.

POPEYE'S SPINACH CROQUETTES
YIELD: 8 SERVINGS, 4 PIECES EACH

★ ★ ★

1 pkg. frozen chopped spinach
1 c. dry bread crumbs
1 egg, beaten or 1/4 c. liquid
   egg substitute
1/4 c. minced onion
1/4 tsp. garlic powder
1/4 c. margarine, melted
1/4 c. Parmesan cheese
1/8 tsp. pepper

Cook spinach and drain well. Combine with other ingredients and form into 1 inch balls and place on lightly greased baking sheet. Place in freezer for 20 minutes until firm. Bake at 325° F. for 25 to 30 minutes.

Calories per serving: 147
Fat: 8 gm. Cholesterol: 22 mg.
Sodium: 247 mg.
For exchange diets, count: 1 bread/starch, 1 1/2 fat

Preparation time: 60 min.

TOMATO POCKETS
YIELD: 8 SERVINGS, 2 PIECES EACH

★ ★ ★

16 cherry tomatoes, cleaned
1/4 c. chopped celery
1 c. chopped cooked chicken
   pieces
1 TB. pimiento
1 TB. chopped almonds
1/4 c. lite mayonnaise
12 toothpicks

Use a sharp knife to cut off the top 1/4 of the tomato. Scoop out the inside and discard. Combine remaining ingredients and stuff inside. Replace the tomato top and secure with a toothpick.

Calories per serving: 78
Fat: 4 gm. Cholesterol: 20 mg.
Sodium: 43 mg.
For exchange diets, count: 1 vegetable, 1 fat

Preparation time: 15 min.

WRAPPED CARROTS
YIELD: 4 SERVINGS, 4 PIECES EACH

★ ★ ★

---

4 medium carrots, cleaned
and peeled

1/2 c. lite mayonnaise

2 TB. dry buttermilk salad
dressing mix

16 slices of thinly sliced lean
turkey or dried beef

16 toothpicks

Cut the carrots into 4 pieces. Combine the mayonnaise and dressing mix. Dip each piece of carrot into the dressing and roll up in slices of dried beef or turkey. Secure with a toothpick.

Calories per 4 pieces: 111
Fat: 8 gm. Cholesterol: 21 mg.
Sodium: 141 mg. (using turkey)
For exchange diets, count: 1 vegetable, 1 lean meat, 1 fat

Preparation time: 15 min.

Baked Potato Burrito
Yield: 8 servings

★ ★ ★

4 potatoes	1/4 tsp. salt
1 TB. vegetable oil	1 lb. lean hamburger
1 c. chopped onions	1 TB. tomato paste
1/2 tsp. garlic powder	1/2 c. bottled salsa
2 tsp. chili powder	3 c. shredded lettuce
2 tsp. cumin	3 tomatoes, cubed
1/2 tsp. oregano	1 oz. part-skim cheddar
1/2 tsp. pepper	cheese, shredded

Bake potatoes in MICROWAVE (8 to12 minutes on high power, turning once during cooking). Cool, then slice in half lengthwise. Scoop out half the pulp from each piece and set aside. Meanwhile, heat oil over medium heat in a large skillet. Add onions and saute 5 minutes. Add spices and cook 1 minute. Add ground beef and cook until browned. Pour mixture into a collander and drain off all fat, pressing meat to promote draining. Stir in reserved potato pulp, tomato paste, and salsa. Stuff the potato shells with prepared meat filling. Place on a baking sheet, and cover with cheese. Broil 6 to 8 minutes until cheese is melted. Serve with lettuce and tomatoes on the side.

Calories per potato half: 232
Fat: 6 gm. Cholesterol: 36 mg.
Sodium: 238 mg.
For exchange diets, count 1 1/2 lean meat,
1 bread/starch, 3 vegetable

Preparation time: 45 min.

BEAN 'N BACON CASSEROLE
YIELD: 8 1 1/2-C. SERVINGS

★ ★ ★

8 slices bacon, broiled and
   crumbled
1/3 c. sugar
2 TB. cornstarch
3/4 c. vinegar
1/2 c. water
1 16-oz. can no added salt
   green beans
1 16-oz. can lima beans
1 16-oz. can wax beans
1 15-oz. can kidney beans
1 15-oz. can garbanzo beans

Combine sugar, cornstarch, vinegar, and water with whisk in a
medium-sized skillet. Cook and stir to boiling. Drain all the
beans well. Add the beans to the skillet, just stirring to mix.
Simmer for 20 minutes. Stir in crumbled bacon and serve. This
casserole can be prepared and frozen for later use.

Calories per 1 1/2-c. serving: 255
Fat: 4 gm. Cholesterol: 6 mg.
Sodium: 411 mg.
For exchange diets, count: 1 1/2 bread/starch,
1 vegetable, 2 lean meat

Preparation time: 30 min.

FETTUCINE LOW-FAT ALFREDO
YIELD: 8 SERVINGS, 1 C. EACH

★ ★ ★

8 oz. fettucine, cooked tender

4 c. vegetables cut into bite-sized pieces (such as broccoli, carrots, red pepper, pea pods, zucchini, mushrooms, and onions)

1 tsp. margarine

1/4 tsp. garlic powder

1 c. part-skim Ricotta cheese

2 TB. Parmesan cheese

2 TB. skim milk

1 egg or 1/4 c. liquid egg substitute

1/4 tsp. salt (optional)

1/2 tsp. oregano

1/8 tsp. pepper

Cook fettucine according to package directions. Meanwhile, MICROWAVE vegetables in a covered dish with 1 TB. water for 3 minutes. At the same time, melt margarine in a saucepan and add garlic powder. Stir to mix. Blend in cheeses, skim milk, egg, and seasonings. Bring to a boil, reduce heat to low, and cook for 3 minutes. Transfer this sauce to a blender and blend smooth. Drain noodles and vegetables well. Transfer to serving bowl. Pour sauce over noodles and vegetables and toss gently. Serve.

Calories per 1-c. serving: 200
Fat: 6 gm. Cholesterol: 43 mg. with egg; 11 mg. with substitute
Sodium: 137 mg. with salt; 75 mg. without salt
For exchange diets, count: 1 skim milk,
1 bread/starch, 1 fat

Preparation time: 30 min.

HARVEST CASSEROLE WITH WILD RICE
YIELD: 8 1 1/4-C. SERVINGS

★ ★ ★

1 small can Campbell's Special Request Cream of Mushroom Soup

1 15-oz. can no added salt chicken broth

1 jar chopped pimento

1 tsp. parsley

2 tsp. marjoram

1 tsp. thyme

1/2 tsp. pepper

2 c. wild rice

1 medium onion, chopped

1 medium pepper, chopped

8 oz. mushrooms, sliced

1 lb. lean ground pork, browned

1 c. celery, chopped

Brown pork in a large skillet and drain. Add onion, pepper, mushrooms, and celery and cook until vegetables are tender. Add uncooked wild rice, soup, no added salt chicken broth, and seasonings. Mix well, then pour into a 3-qt. casserole and cover. Bake 1 3/4 hours at 325° F. or MICROWAVE at 70% power for 30 minutes, stirring twice during the cooking period. This can be doubled and frozen for later use.

Calories per 1 1/4-c. serving: 313
Fat: 12 gm. Cholesterol: 42 mg.
Sodium: 210 mg.
For exchange diets, count: 2 lean meats,
2 bread/starch, 1 fat

Preparation time: 45 min.

HOPPIN' JOHN
YIELD: 8 1-C. SERVINGS

★ ★ ★

> 1 c. dried black-eyed peas or
> 16-oz. can precooked black-
> eyed peas
> 1 medium onion, chopped
> 3/4 c. chopped celery
> 1 bay leaf
> 3 c. water
> 1/2 tsp. black pepper
> 1 c. uncooked rice
> 2 c. cubed lean cooked ham

In 3-qt. saucepan, combine dried peas, onion, celery, bay leaf, water, and pepper. Simmer for 2 hours until peas are tender. If using pre-cooked peas, reduce water to 1 1/2 cups and simmer 15 minutes. Stir in rice, and simmer for 30 minutes more. Stir in ham just before serving, warming through. This may be frozen and reheated for later use.

Calories per 1-c. serving: 156
Fat: 6 gm. Cholesterol: 14 mg.
Sodium: 588 mg.
For exchange diets, count: 1 bread/starch,
1 vegetable, 1 lean meat

Preparation time: 30 min.

Note: To reduce sodium content, use a reduced-sodium ham or substitute lean roast beef or pork.

MARY'S CREAM SOUP SUBSTITUTE
YIELD: EQUIVALENT OF 10 CANS OF SOUP

★ ★ ★

2 c. nonfat dried milk
3/4 c. cornstarch
1/4 c. chicken or beef bouillon
  particles
2 TB. dried minced onion
1 tsp. thyme
1 tsp. basil
1/2 tsp. pepper

Mix ingredients together and store in a covered container. Use as
a substitute for creamed soups in casserole recipes. To use, mix
1 1/4 c. cold water with 1/3 c. of mix in a small saucepan. Add
1 tsp. margarine. Cook until thickened and substitute for 1 15-oz.
can of cream soup.

Calories per 1/3-c. mix: 94
Fat: less than 1 gm. Cholesterol: 3 mg.
Sodium: 112 mg.
To reduce sodium, use low-sodium bouillon.
For exchange diets, count: 1 bread/starch

Preparation time: 15 min.

MEXICAN CORN MAIN DISH
YIELD: 8 3/4-C. SERVINGS

★ ★ ★

1 lb. lean ground beef,
    browned
4 ears fresh corn or
1 10-oz. package frozen corn,
    thawed
1 egg or 1/4 c. liquid egg
    substitute
1/2 c. nonfat yogurt
1 c. shredded mozzarella
    cheese
1/2 c. cornmeal
1 7-oz. can diced green chilis
1/4 tsp. garlic powder
1/4 tsp. salt
Chopped fresh parsley, as an
    optional garnish

Preheat oven to 350° F. Brown ground beef; drain well. Spray a
3-qt. casserole dish with nonstick cooking spray. Cut corn off the
cob if necessary. Put yogurt and egg in blender. Puree well.
Combine this with corn, browned meat, and all other ingredients
in casserole dish. Sprinkle fresh parsley over the top as a garnish
Bake for 50 minutes or MICROWAVE on high for 20 minutes.
This casserole is done when the center is firm and the top is
lightly browned. This may be assembled, frozen, and thawed for
later baking.

Calories per 3/4-c. serving: 187
Fat: 5 gm. Cholesterol: 40 mg. with egg; 8 mg. with egg substitute
Sodium: 172 mg. with salt; 109 mg. without
For exchange diets, count: 2 lean meat,
1 bread/starch

Preparation time: 35 min. if microwaved

PIZZA LOAF
YIELD: 8 SLICES

★ ★ ★

1 prepared pizza crust (from refrigerated tube)	1 beaten egg or 1/4 c. liquid egg substitute
1/2 lb. lean ground beef, browned and drained	1 sm. can sliced mushrooms, drained
8 oz. shredded mozzarella cheese	1/2 tsp. oregano
1 8-oz. can no added salt tomato sauce	1 medium onion, sliced thin
	1 lg. pimiento-stuffed olive, cut in half
10 oz. frozen spinach, thawed and squeezed dry	2 TB. Parmesan cheese

Preheat oven to 400° F. Remove pizza dough from tube and cut 1/4 of the dough away and set aside. Spray a loaf pan with nonstick cooking spray and press 3/4 of the pizza dough over the bottom and sides of pan. Place 1/3 of the shredded cheese over the bottom of the dough. Top with meat, sauce and oregano. Combine spinach with egg and spoon over the oregano. Next add remaining cheese, mushrooms, onions, and olives. Use the reserved dough for the top, crimping edges to seal. Slit the top in 3 places and sprinkle with Parmesan. Bake for 45 minutes or until crust is well browned. Remove from oven for 10 minutes before slicing and serving.

Calories per 1 slice: 276
Fat: 11 gm. Cholesterol: 66 mg. with egg; 34 mg.
with egg substitute
Sodium: 422 mg.
For exchange diets, count: 3 lean meat,
1 1/2 bread/starch

Preparation time: 60 min.

PIZZA ROUNDS
YIELD: 8 SERVINGS

★ ★ ★

1 (1 lb.) loaf frozen bread
  dough
1/2 c. no added salt tomato
  sauce
1/2 tsp. basil
1/2 tsp. oregano
1/4 tsp. garlic
1/4 tsp. fennel
3/4 c. shredded mozzarella
  cheese
1/4 c. Parmesan cheese
8 oz. shredded roast beef
1/2 c. onion, chopped

Preheat oven to 375° F. Cover dough and allow to thaw at room
temperature until pliable. Roll dough on a lightly floured board
into a 12-inch square. Spread with no added salt tomato sauce,
sprinkle with seasonings and layer remaining ingredients. Roll
dough up tightly in jelly-roll fashion, pinching the edges to seal.
Cut roll into 8 pieces, and place in muffin tins which have been
sprayed with liquid shortening. Let rise until double in bulk.
Bake for 18 minutes or until browned. Remove from pan and
serve. These may be baked and frozen for later use. If frozen, rewarm for 45 seconds to 1 minute in the MICROWAVE before
serving.

Calories per round: 234
Fat: 5 gm. Cholesterol: 28 mg.
Sodium: 377 mg.
For exchange diets, count: 1 1/2 bread/starch, 2 lean meat

Preparation time: 45 min.

SPINACH AND BACON CRUNCH
YIELD: 4 WEDGES

★ ★ ★

2 strips bacon, cooked, drained and crumbled	8 oz. fresh mushrooms, sliced thin
1/2 c. part-skim Ricotta cheese, blended smooth	2 beaten eggs or 1/2 c. liquid egg substitute
5 oz. evaporated skim milk	10 oz. frozen spinach, thawed and squeezed dry
2 tsp. lemon juice	3 c. Corn or Rice Chex cereal, crushed fine
1/4 tsp. pepper	
1 tsp. onion powder	1 TB. margarine
	1/4 tsp. garlic powder

Preheat oven to 350° F. (Recipe can also be microwaved.) Spray a 2-qt. round baking dish (souffle dish works best) with nonstick cooking spray. Slice mushrooms and saute them in skillet, also sprayed with nonstick spray, until tender. Remove mushrooms and cook bacon until crisp. Drain bacon and blot with paper towel. Crumble bacon. Next, blenderize the Ricotta cheese. In a mixing bowl, mix cheese, milk, beaten eggs, bacon, mushrooms, onion powder, lemon juice, pepper, and spinach until blended. Melt 1 TB. margarine in skillet. Add the crushed cereal and garlic powder, tossing to coat. Sprinkle this over the spinach mixture. Bake 30 to 40 minutes until the mixture is bubbly, or MICROWAVE on high power for 12 to 15 minutes.

Calories per wedge: 270
Fat: 7 gm. Cholesterol: 12 mg. with egg substitute;100 mg. with egg
Sodium: 426 mg.
For exchange diets, count: 2 lean meat,
2 bread/starch

Preparation time: 35 min. if microwaved

TACO CASSEROLE
YIELD: 8 1-C. SERVINGS

★ ★ ★

1 15-oz. can kidney beans, processed smooth in blender	8 oz. no added salt tomato sauce
1 lb. lean ground beef, browned and drained	1/4 c. chopped onion
	1/4 c. chopped green pepper
1/2 tsp. garlic powder	4 medium flour tortillas, cut into triangles
1/2 tsp. cumin	2 oz. part-skim American cheese, grated
1/4 tsp. cayenne (optional)	Chili powder garnish

Preheat oven to 375° F. Spray a 9 x 13-inch dish or two 8 x 8-inch baking dishes with nonstick cooking spray. Spread processed beans onto bottom of prepared pan. Combine browned meat with garlic, cumin, cayenne, and tomato sauce. Spread over beans. Top with onion, green pepper, tortilla triangles, and cheese. Sprinkle chili powder on top. Bake for 30 minutes or MICROWAVE for 20 to 22 minutes on medium-high power. Remove from oven and let stand for 5 minutes. Serve with chopped lettuce and tomato. This may be assembled and frozen for later baking.

Calories per 1-c. serving: 246
Fat: 7 gm. Cholesterol: 19 mg.
Sodium: 192 mg.
For exchange diets, count: 1 bread/starch,
2 vegetable, 2 lean meat

Preparation time: 40 min.

TORTILLA CHICKEN BRUNCH
YIELD: 8 4-IN. SQ. SERVINGS

★ ★ ★

8 7-in. flour tortillas
1 1/2 lb. chicken pieces,
  browned
4 oz. part-skim cheddar
  cheese, shredded
8 eggs, slightly beaten or 2 c.
  liquid egg substitute
3 c. skim milk
1/8 tsp. salt (optional)
1/2 tsp. chili powder
1/2 tsp. cumin
1/4 c. chopped scallions

Preheat oven to 325° F. Arrange tortillas to cover the bottom and sides of a 13 x 9-inch baking dish sprayed with nonstick cooking spray. It may be necessary to cut the tortillas in half. Sprinkle with chicken and cheese. Combine eggs, milk, and seasonings with a whisk. Pour over chicken and cheese. Sprinkle the top with scallions. Bake for 40 to 50 minutes until knife inserted in center comes out clean.

Calories per serving: 294
Fat: 11 gm. Cholesterol: 322 mg.
Sodium: 410 mg. with salt; 377 mg. without salt
For exchange diets, count: 3 lean meat,
1 1/2 bread/starch

Preparation time: 50 min.

TUNA AND NOODLE CASSEROLE
YIELD: 4 1 1/2-C. SERVINGS

★ ★ ★

4 oz. noodles of choice, cooked according to package directions	1 c. plain low-fat yogurt
	1 TB. flour
	1/4 tsp. marjoram
4 oz. fresh mushrooms, sliced thin	1/4 tsp. thyme
	1/4 tsp. salt (optional)
1/2 c. green onion, chopped fine	1/2 tsp. white pepper
1 TB. margarine	1 TB. lemon juice
1 small can sliced water chestnuts, drained	1/2 c. chow mein noodles
1 small can water-packed tuna, drained	

Preheat oven to 350° F. Cook noodles according to package directions. Do not overcook. Meanwhile, saute onions and mushrooms in margarine. Combine cooked noodles, vegetables, and tuna in an 8-inch square baking dish sprayed with nonstick cooking spray. Combine yogurt, flour, marjoram, thyme, salt, pepper, and lemon juice. Fold into the tuna mixture. Top with chow mein noodles. Bake for 30 minutes or MICROWAVE for 18 to 20 minutes until bubbly. This recipe can be assembled, frozen. To serve later, defrost in microwave for 15 minutes, then bake at 350° F. for 30 minutes or MICROWAVE on high power 18 to 20 minutes.

Calories per 1 1/.2-c. serving: 299
Fat: 7 gm. Cholesterol: 16 mg.
Sodium: 186 mg. with salt; 62 mg. without salt
For exchange diets, count: 3 lean meat,
3 bread/starch

Preparation time: 40 min.

TUNA STUFFED MANICOTTI
YIELD: 4 SERVINGS, 2 SHELLS EACH

★ ★ ★

8 cooked manicotti shells	*Sauce:*
2 5-oz. cans water packed tuna, drained	1/2 c. nonfat cottage cheese, blended smooth
1/2 c. nonfat cottage cheese	1/2 c. plain nonfat yogurt
1 TB. dried parsley	1/4 tsp. dill weed
1/4 c. diced onions	1/8 tsp. garlic powder
1 tsp. lemon juice	
1/4 tsp. dill weed	*Topping:*
	2 TB. Parmesan cheese

Cook manicotti according to package directions. Drain and cool.
Combine tuna, cottage cheese, parsley, onions, lemon juice, and
dill weed in a small mixing bowl. Stuff manicotti shells with tuna
mixture and place seam side down in a 7 x 11-inch baking dish
sprayed with nonstick cooking spray. Combine ingredients for
the sauce and spoon over manicotti. Sprinkle with Parmesan
cheese. Bake at 350° F. for 30 minutes or MICROWAVE for 8
minutes on high power.

Calories per serving: 285
Fat: 3 gm. Cholesterol: 76 mg.
Sodium: 327 mg.
For exchange diets, count: 2 lean meat,
1 bread/starch, 1 skim milk

Preparation time: 25 min. if microwaved

TURKEY AND MUSHROOM TETRAZZINI
YIELD: 4 1 1/2-C. SERVINGS

★ ★ ★

3 oz. spaghetti, cooked tender
1 TB. margarine
2 TB. flour
1/8 tsp. salt
1/4 tsp. pepper
1 c. no added salt chicken
    broth
1/2 c. skim milk
1 TB. sherry
8 oz. fresh mushrooms, sliced
    thin
1 c. cooked turkey, cut into
    chunks
1/4 c. Parmesan cheese

Cook spaghetti by package directions and drain. Preheat oven to 350° F. In Dutch oven, saute mushrooms in 1 tsp. margarine. Remove to a 2-qt. casserole dish sprayed with nonstick cooking spray. Melt remaining 2 tsp. margarine over medium heat and add flour, salt, pepper, broth, and milk, stirring until mixture thickens. Add the cooked sauce, cooked spaghetti, mushrooms, sherry, and turkey to the casserole dish. Blend. Sprinkle with Parmesan cheese. Bake for 30 minutes or MICROWAVE for 14 minutes on high power.

Calories per 1 1/2-c. serving: 269
Fat: 9 gm. Cholesterol: 48 mg.
Sodium: 239 mg.
For exchange diets, count: 1 1/2 bread/starch, 3 lean meat

Preparation time: 35 min.

TURKEY CREPES
YIELD: 8 CREPES

★ ★ ★

> *Crepes:*
> 2/3 c. skim milk
> 2/3 c. flour
> 1 egg or 1/4 c. liquid egg
>   substitute
> 1 TB. margarine, melted

Blend ingredients smooth with rotary beater. Pour 1 tsp. oil into a 6-inch skillet. Over a medium flame, heat oil, tipping to cover the pan. Add 2 TB. batter to skillet and cook until the bottom is browned. Turn over to brown the other side. Place crepes between layers of wax paper on a plate.

Filling:	
2 TB. celery, diced	1 2/3 c. skim milk
2 TB. onion, diced	1/4 c. orange juice concentrate
1 TB. margarine	2 tsp. dried parsley
1/4 c. flour	1 1/2 c. chopped cooked
Dash ground black pepper	turkey
	3/4 c. seedless green grapes

Saute onion and celery in margarine. Add flour and pepper and gradually stir in milk, stirring until thick. Add the juice concentrate and parsley. Pour half of this sauce into a pitcher. Add the turkey and grapes to the remaining half of the sauce. Stir. Use the turkey mixture to fill crepes, rolling up and placing seam side down in a 7 x 11-inch baking pan sprayed with nonstick cooking spray. Pour reserved sauce over the crepes and bake 20 minutes at 350° F. or MICROWAVE for 10 minutes on high power.

Calories per serving: 207
Fat: 5 gm. Cholesterol: 41 mg.
Sodium: 115 mg.
For exchange diets, count: 2 lean meat, 1 bread/starch, 1 vegetable

Preparation time: 50 min.

TURKEY SALAD A LA ORANGE
YIELD: 4 1-C. SERVINGS

★ ★ ★

1 1/2 c. cooked turkey, cut
  into small pieces

1 c. sliced celery

1 TB. red onion, diced fine

1 orange, peeled and cut into
  1/2-inch pieces

Dressing:

3 TB. orange juice
  concentrate

1 tsp. vegetable oil

1 TB. sugar

1 TB. vinegar

1/8 tsp. dry mustard

Dash tabasco sauce (optional)

2 TB. light mayonnaise or
  salad dressing

Combine first four ingredients for salad in a salad bowl. In a shaker container, combine all ingredients (except mayonnaise) for the dressing. When well blended, use a whisk to blend in the mayonnaise. Pour over salad and serve on a bed of fresh greens.

Calories per 1-c. serving: 222
Fat: 7 gm. Cholesterol: 69 mg.
Sodium: 122 mg.
For exchange diets, count: 2 lean meat,
1/2 bread/starch, 1 fruit

Preparation time: 15 min.

VEGETABLE ENCHILADAS
YIELD: 4 SERVINGS, 1 TORTILLA EACH

★ ★ ★

4 flour tortillas
1 c. shredded part-skim
    Monterey Jack cheese
1/2 c. part-skim Ricotta
    cheese
1/2 tsp. chili powder
1/4 tsp. cumin
1 c. tomato chunks
1/2 c. shredded zucchini
1/2 c. shredded carrots
1/3 c. chopped green pepper
1/4 c. chopped onion
1/2 c. chunky salsa sauce

Preheat oven to 350° F. (Recipe can be microwaved.) Combine
tomato, zucchini, carrots, pepper, and onion in a 1-qt. baking dish
and cover. Steam for 4 minutes in the MICROWAVE.
Meanwhile, combine the cheese, chili powder, and cumin. Spread
the cheese mixture over the tortillas. Spoon vegetable mixture on
top. Roll up the tortillas and place seam side down in an 8-inch
square baking dish sprayed with nonstick cooking spray. Pour
the salsa over the top and bake for 25 minutes or MICROWAVE
for 7 minutes on high power until bubbly.

Calories per serving: 251
Fat: 9 gm. Cholesterol: 26 mg.
Sodium: 348 mg.
For exchange diets, count: 2 bread/starch,
1 lean meat, 1 fat

Preparation time: 20 min. if microwaved

BEEFY MUSHROOM AND BARLEY SOUP
YIELD: 8 SERVINGS, 1-C. EACH

★ ★ ★

2 1/2 c. sliced mushrooms
1/2 c. chopped onion
2 TB. margarine
1/3 c. flour
6 c. water
1 lb. lean stew beef cubes
2 c. skim milk
1/2 c. quick pearled barley
1 TB. dry sherry
2 tsp. Worcestershire sauce
1 TB. dried parsley
1/4 tsp. pepper

In a 2-qt. kettle, simmer 1 lb. stew beef in 6 c. water for 15 minutes. In skillet, saute mushrooms and onion in margarine. Stir in flour and gradually add milk, stirring until thick. Transfer this to the kettle of beef and stock, stirring to blend. Stir in barley and seasonings. Simmer for 15 minutes. This may be prepared and frozen for later use.

Calories per 1-c. serving: 253
Fat: 9 gm. Cholesterol: 29 mg.
Sodium: 126 mg.
For exchange diets, count: 3 lean meat, 1 1/2 bread starch

Preparation time: 45 min.

CALIFORNIA BLEND CREAM SOUP
YIELD: 4 1 1/2 c.-SERVINGS

★ ★ ★

1 TB. margarine

1 c. chopped onion

2 tsp. dried parsley

10 oz. frozen California blend vegetables (carrots, broccoli, and cauliflower or use vegetable of choice)

14 oz. no added salt chicken broth

2 TB. flour

1/4 tsp. pepper

1 c. skim milk

1/4 tsp. grated lemon peel

1/4 c. (or 2 oz.) soft cheddar cheese spread (such as Cheeze Whiz®)

In a 2-qt. stockpot, saute onion in margarine. Add parsley, vegetables, and broth. In shaker container, combine flour and pepper with milk. Slowly whisk the milk into the vegetables and broth. Heat just until boiling. Add lemon peel and cheese. Reduce heat. Do not allow milk-based soups to come to a rolling boil or they will lose their creamy consistency.

Calories per 1 1/2-c. serving: 137
Fat: 6 gm. Cholesterol: 12 mg.
Sodium: 298 mg.
For exchange diets, count: 1 skim milk, 1 fat

Preparation time: 20 min.

CHICKEN AND RICE SOUP
YIELD: 8 1 1/2-C. SERVINGS

★ ★ ★

2 qt. no added salt chicken broth
2 c. diced cooked chicken
1/4 tsp. salt
1/2 c. celery
2 scallions, chopped
2 carrots, peeled and sliced thin
3 whole cloves
1/2 tsp. nutmeg
1 tsp. dried parsley
1 bay leaf
1 c. frozen peas
1 c. sliced fresh mushrooms
1/2 c. quick rice (dry)

Combine all ingredients in a 4-qt. stockpot. Bring to a boil, reduce to simmer, and cover. Ready in 30 minutes.

Calories per 1 1/2-c. serving: 135
Fat: 2 gm. Cholesterol: 45 mg.
Sodium: 102 mg.
For exchange diets, count: 1 1/2 lean meat,
2 vegetable

Preparation time: 30 min.

Note: Instead of using canned chicken broth, you can make your own by stewing a chicken and removing the fat from the stock.

CHRISTMAS BISQUE
YIELD: 8 1-C. SERVINGS

★ ★ ★

2 TB. liquid oil margarine

1 small onion, diced

1 carrot, sliced

1 stalk celery, sliced

12 oz. cod, thawed and cut into small pieces

12 oz. white wine

12 oz. no added salt chicken broth

2 TB. flour

2 c. evaporated skim milk

1/2 tsp. paprika

1/4 c. scallion tops, finely chopped

Melt liquid oil margarine in a 3-qt. heavy saucepan. Add onion, carrot, and celery, and cook for 5 minutes. Stir in cod, wine, and chicken broth. Simmer for 15 minutes, until cod is white and flaky. Combine evaporated skim milk and flour in a shaker container; then slowly whisk into heated mixture. Bring just to a boil, then reduce heat and simmer for 3 minutes, stirring continuously. Ladle bisque into serving bowls and sprinkle with paprika and scallion tops.

Calories per 1-c. serving: 165
Fat: 4 gm. Cholesterol: 25 mg.
Sodium: 151 mg.
For exchange diets, count: 1 skim milk, 1 vegetable, 1 lean meat

Preparation time: 30 min.

CHUNKY BEEF CHILI
YIELD: 8 1 1/2-c. SERVINGS

★ ★ ★

1 lb. stew beef, trimmed and
  browned
1 c. onion, chopped
1/2 c. green pepper, chopped
1/4 c. celery, chopped
1 TB. vegetable oil
1 16-oz. can no added salt
  tomatoes
1 8-oz. can no added salt
  tomato sauce
1/2 tsp. thyme
1/4 tsp. garlic powder
1/2 tsp. sugar
1/4 tsp. oregano
1 TB. chili powder
1 15-oz. can chili beans

Saute onion, pepper, and celery in oil in a 3-qt. stockpot. When
vegetables are tender, add cooked meat and all remaining
ingredients. Bring to a boil, reduce heat to a simmer, and cover.
Ready in 20 minutes.

Calories per 1 1/2-c. serving: 208
Fat: 7 gm. Cholesterol: 15 mg.
Sodium: 37 mg.
For exchange diets, count: 2 lean meat,
1 bread/starch

Preparation time: 20 min.

COCK-A-LEEKIE SOUP
YIELD: 4 2-C. SERVINGS

★ ★ ★

1/2 c. barley
1 lb. uncooked chicken pieces
2 qt. no added salt chicken
  broth
1/4 tsp. salt (optional)
6 peppercorns
1 bay leaf
1 TB. dried parsely
1/4 tsp. ground cloves
6 leeks (1 lb.)
1 tea bag

In a 3-qt. soup kettle, steam 1 lb. raw chicken pieces in 2 qt. no added salt chicken broth for 20 minutes. (Or steam a 3-lb. whole chicken in 2 qt. water, deboning the meat and saving the broth. Be sure to remove the fat from the top of the reserved broth.) Add barley, salt, bay leaf, parsley, cloves, and sliced leeks to the chicken and broth. Remove the tea from the bag and tie peppercorns securely inside. Add this to soup and bring to a boil. Reduce heat to simmer and cook for 30 to 45 minutes more. Remove peppercorns before serving.

Calories per 2-c. serving: 318
Fat: 6 gm. Cholesterol: 65 mg.
Sodium: 213 mg. with salt; 97 mg. without salt
For exchange diets, count: 4 lean meat,
1 bread/starch, 1 vegetable

Preparation time: 50 min.

IRISH POTATO SOUP
YIELD: 4 1-C. SERVINGS

★ ★ ★

> 4 medium potatoes, peeled
>   and cubed fine
> 1/4 c. chopped onion
> 1/4 c. chopped celery
> 1/4 c. grated carrots
> 1/4 tsp. salt (optional)
> 1/2 c. no added salt chicken
>   broth
> 1/4 c. flour
> 1 TB. margarine, melted
> 2 c. skim milk
> Fresh parsley

In a 2-qt. kettle or microwave dish, steam vegetables with broth and optional salt until tender. Combine flour, margarine, and milk in shaker container. Stir into vegetables, bring to a boil, and then reduce to simmer for 5 minutes. Ladle into bowls and garnish with fresh parsley.

Calories per 1-c. serving: 186
Fat: 4 gm. Cholesterol: 4 mg.
Sodium: 236 mg. with salt; 113 mg. without salt
For exchange diets, count: 2 bread/starch, 1 fat

Preparation time: 25 min.

MICHIGAN BEAN SOUP
YIELD: 8 1-C. SERVINGS

* * *

1 1/2 c. dry or 24-oz. can navy beans	1 c. carrots, diced
6 c. water	2 whole cloves
1 TB. margarine	2 bay leaves
1 c. chopped onions	4 c. no added salt beef or chicken broth
8 oz. lean ham, cubed	1/4 tsp. pepper
1/4 tsp. garlic powder	2 TB. cider vinegar
2 c. celery, chopped	

When using dry beans, pour enough water over beans to cover well in a one-gallon kettle. Soak overnight. Pour off the water and drain beans in a colander. Saute onion, ham, and garlic in margarine until onion is tender. In a 1-gallon stockpot, combine beans, sauteed ingredients, and all other ingredients except vinegar. Simmer for 4 hours with dried beans or 20 minutes with canned beans. Add vinegar just before serving. This may be prepared and frozen for later thawing and reheating.

Calories per 1-c. serving: 210
Fat: 4 gm. Cholesterol: 31 mg.
Sodium: 292 mg.
For exchange diets, count: 2 bread/starch,
1 1/2 lean meat

Preparation time: 30 min. using canned beans

Speed Alert: If dry beans are used, allow overnight soaking and then 4 1/2 hr. cooking time.

MICROWAVE MINESTRONE
YIELD: 4 1 1/2-C. SERVINGS

★ ★ ★

1/4 c. water
1/2 c. chopped onion
1/2 c. chopped celery
1/4 tsp. garlic powder
16 oz. no added salt chunky
 tomatoes
1 c. fine noodles
1 c. sliced cabbage
1 1/2 tsp. low-sodium beef
 bouillon powder
1/2 tsp. basil
1/2 tsp. oregano
1 1/2 c. water
1/2 lb. fully cooked turkey
 sausage, sliced thin

Place onion, celery, and garlic powder with 1/4 c. water in a 3-qt. microwave dish. Cover and MICROWAVE on high power for 3 minutes. Add remaining ingredients except for sausage, stirring to blend. Cover and MICROWAVE on high power for 15 minutes, or until the noodles are tender, stirring twice. Stir in sausage. Cover and let stand for 10 minutes. Serve.

Calories per 1 1/2-c. serving: 227
Fat: 3 gm. Cholesterol: 40 mg.
Sodium: 61 mg.
For exchange diets, count: 2 vegetable,
1 bread/starch, 2 lean meat

Preparation time: 30 min.

PORK AND VEGETABLE STEW
YIELD: 8 1-c. SERVINGS

★ ★ ★

1 15-oz. can great northern beans	1 10-oz. pkg. frozen cut green beans, thawed
1 8-oz. can no added salt tomato sauce	1 10-oz. pkg. frozen sliced zucchini, thawed
1 10 1/2-oz. can no added salt beef broth	1/2 tsp. ground sage
2 TB. cornstarch	1/2 tsp. marjoram
1/2 c. chopped onions	1/2 tsp. garlic powder
1 lb. pork steak, cut into 1/2-inch cubes	1 bay leaf

In a skillet, brown pork with sliced onion. In a Dutch oven, stir tomato sauce, broth, and cornstarch with a whisk until smooth. Add beans, zucchini, pork, and seasonings to liquids. Bring to a boil, stirring until mixture thickens. Reduce heat and simmer for 15 minutes. TO MICROWAVE: Use a 3-qt. casserole dish and MICROWAVE all ingredients except pork and onions on high power for 15 minutes, stopping 3 times to stir. Stir in browned pork and onions, cover, and microwave on medium (or 50%) power for 3 minutes. This stew freezes well.

Calories per 1-c. serving: 219
Fat: 8 gm. Cholesterol: 47 mg.
Sodium: 179 mg.
For exchange diets, count:
2 lean meat, 1 vegetable, and 1 bread/starch

Preparation time: 25 min.

PUMPKIN SOUP
YIELD: 4 1 1/2-C. SERVINGS

★ ★ ★

1 TB. margarine
1 c. chopped onion
1/2 c. sliced celery
1/4 tsp. garlic powder
1/4 tsp. salt
1/2 tsp. white pepper
3 c. no added salt chicken broth
1 16-oz. can solid pack pumpkin
1 c. evaporated skim milk
2 scallions, finely chopped

In 2-qt. saucepan, melt margarine. Add onion, celery, and garlic powder, cooking until vegetables are soft. Add broth, salt, and pepper and simmer for 15 minutes. Stir in pumpkin and evaporated skim milk. Cook for 5 minutes, then pour into a blender container and blenderize on low speed about 30 seconds until creamy. Ladle into soup bowls. Top with chopped scallions, and serve.

Calories per 1 1/2-c. serving: 120
Fat: less than 1 gm. Cholesterol: 2 mg.
Sodium: 215 mg.
For exchange diets, count: 1 bread/starch, 2 vegetable

Preparation time: 30 min.

Shopper's Chili
Yield: 8 1 1/2-c. servings

* * *

Put this in the crockpot while you go shopping.

1 1/2 lb. lean ground beef
1/4 tsp. garlic powder
1 28-oz. can no added salt tomatoes, undrained
2 medium onions, chopped
1 medium green pepper, diced
1 15-oz. can no added salt tomato sauce
1 1/2 c. water
1/4 c. chili powder
1 stalk celery, diced
1 1/2 tsp. pepper
1/2 tsp. salt (optional)
1 bay leaf
1 15-oz. can red kidney beans, drained, and rinsed

Brown meat in microwave or skillet. Drain well, and transfer to a crockpot or slow cooker. Add all remaining ingredients and slow cook 4 to 8 hours, uncovered. Remove bay leaf before serving.

Calories per 1 1/2-c. serving: 275
Fat: 11 gm. Cholesterol: 63 mg.
Sodium: 428 mg. with salt; 306 mg. without salt
For exchange diets, count:
3 lean meat, 1vegetable, 1 bread/starch

Preparation time: 4-8 hours in crockpot

Speed Alert: Recipe requires 4 to 8 hours.

232

SPICY CHICKEN STEW
YIELD: 4 1 1/2-C. SERVINGS

★ ★ ★

8 oz. raw chicken pieces
1 TB. vegetable oil
1 onion, chopped
2 TB. chili powder
1 16-oz. can no added salt
   tomatoes
1 4-oz. can chopped green
   chilies
1 c. water
1 16-oz. can black beans
6 oz. frozen whole kernel corn
1 TB. dried parsley
1/4 tsp. salt, optional

Saute chicken pieces and onion in oil in a Dutch oven until chicken is browned. Add all remaining ingredients and bring to a boil. Reduce heat to a simmer and cook 15 more minutes. This recipe can be prepared and frozen for later. Thaw, reheat, and serve.

Calories per 1 1/2-c. serving: 330
Fat: 2 gm. Cholesterol: 32 mg.
Sodium: 195 mg. with salt; 81 mg. without salt
For exchange diets, count: 2 lean meat, 2 vegetable, 2 bread/starch

Preparation time: 25 min.

VEGETABLE CHOWDER WITH BACON
YIELD: 4 1 1/2-C. SERVINGS

★ ★ ★

6 slices bacon, broiled and
  crumbled
1 sm. can no added salt
  chicken broth
2 c. finely chopped potatoes
1 c. shredded carrots
1/2 c. chopped onion
1/2 tsp. curry powder
1/8 tsp. pepper
1 12-oz. can evaporated skim
  milk

Broil bacon until crisp; then tear into pieces. Meanwhile, in 3-qt.
kettle, combine broth and vegetables. Steam vegetables until
tender. Stir in curry, pepper, broiled bacon pieces, and
evaporated skim milk. Heat through, about 10 minutes over
medium heat. Do not boil!

Calories per 1 1/2-c. serving: 243
Fat: 5 gm. Cholesterol: 11 mg.
Sodium: 304 mg.
For exchange diets, count: 1 vegetable,
2 bread/starch, 1 fat

Preparation time: 25 min.

AUTUMN MORNING BUNS
YIELD: 12 BUNS

★ ★ ★

1/2 c. chopped almonds
1/2 c. liquid vegetable oil
1/2 c. brown sugar
1 tsp. light corn syrup
1 c. flour
1 c. whole wheat flour
1 TB. baking powder
1 tsp. cinnamon
1/4 tsp. salt
2 eggs or 1/2 c. liquid egg substitute
1 c. skim milk
1 tsp. vanilla
1/4 tsp. almond extract
1/2 tsp. grated orange peel
1/4 c. dates

Preheat oven to 375° F. Spray 12 muffin cups with nonstick cooking spray. Sprinkle almonds evenly into muffin cups. Sprinkle 2 TB. brown sugar over almonds. In mixing bowl, beat vegetable oil, remaining 6 TB. of brown sugar and light corn syrup together. Sift dry ingredients together. In small mixing bowl, beat eggs, skim milk, vanilla, and almond extract together. Add dry ingredients and egg mixture alternately with sugar mixture, beating well after each addition. Fold in orange peel and dates. Pour into prepared muffin cups. Bake for 20 to 25 minutes until browned on top. Cool for 5 minutes only, then invert muffin tin onto plate, and allow buns to fall gently out. The tops of the buns will be crusty.

Calories per bun: 184
Fat: 4 gm.   Cholesterol: 46 mg. with egg
Sodium: 70 mg.
For exchange diets, count: 2 bread/starch, 1 fat

Preparation time: 50 min.

CARROT MUFFINS
YIELD: 12 MUFFINS

★ ★ ★

1 c. flour
1 c. whole wheat flour
1/4 c. brown sugar
2 tsp. baking powder
2 tsp. cinnamon
1/4 tsp. salt
1 tsp. grated orange peel
1/2 c. orange juice
1/2 c. skim milk
1/4 c. liquid vegetable oil
1 egg or 1/4 c. liquid egg
   substitute
1 c. grated carrot

Preheat oven to 400° F. Mix flours, sugar, baking powder, cinnamon, and salt in large bowl. Put orange peel, juice, milk, oil, and egg in medium-size bowl. Beat until smooth. Stir in carrot. Pour over dry ingredients and stir just until moist. Spoon batter into muffin cups 3/4 full. Bake for 20 minutes.

Calories: 144
Fat: 5 gm. Cholesterol: 23 mg. with egg
Sodium: 99 mg.
For exchange diets, count: 1 bread/starch,
1 vegetable, 1 fat

Preparation time: 40 min.

CATHY'S CHEESE PEPPER BREAD
YIELD: 16 SLICES

★ ★ ★

Cathy Carlyle gets the compliments for this recipe.

> 1 pkg. (quick type) active dry yeast
>
> 1/4 c. hot tap water
>
> 2 1/3 c. flour
>
> 2 TB. sugar
>
> 1/8 tsp. salt
>
> 1/4 tsp. baking soda
>
> 1 c. nonfat cottage cheese
>
> 1 egg or 1/4 c. liquid egg substitute
>
> 1 c. shredded part-skim (or light) American cheese
>
> 1/2 tsp. coarse ground pepper

Preheat oven to 350° F. Spray two 1-lb. coffee cans or 1 loaf pan with nonstick cooking spray. In large mixing bowl, dissolve yeast in hot water. Add 1 1/3 c. flour, sugar, salt, soda, cottage cheese, and egg. Blend 1/2 minute on low speed, scraping bowl constantly, then 2 minutes on high speed, scraping bowl occasionally. Stir in remaining flour, cheese, and pepper. Blend well. Pour batter in pans and let rise 35 to 50 minutes. Bake 40 minutes or until golden brown. Cool 5 minutes. Remove from pans, and cool on rack.

Calories per 1 slice serving: 97
Fat: 2 gm. Cholesterol: 29 mg. with egg
Sodium: 242 mg.
For exchange diets, count: 1 bread/starch,
1 lean meat

Preparation time: 2 hours

Speed Alert: Recipe takes 2 hours.

CRANAPPLE BREAD
YIELD: 12 SLICES

★ ★ ★

1 c. fresh or frozen
   cranberries, chopped fine
1/4 c. sugar
1 3/4 c. flour
1/3 c. sugar
1 TB. baking powder
3/4 tsp. cinnamon
1/4 tsp. allspice
1/2 tsp. salt
1 egg, beaten or 1/4 c. liquid
   egg substitute
1/3 c. vegetable oil
1 c. applesauce
1/4 c. walnuts

Preheat oven to 350° F. Chop cranberries and sprinkle with 1/4 c.
sugar and set aside. Combine dry ingredients in a mixing bowl.
Beat egg, oil, and applesauce together in a separate bowl and add
to dry ingredients, stirring well. Gently fold in nuts and
cranberry mixture. Spray 1 large loaf pan with nonstick cooking
spray and pour batter into the pan. Bake 35 minutes or until
toothpick inserted in center comes out clean.

Calories per 1 slice serving: 166
Fat: 7 gm. Cholesterol: 14 mg. with egg
Sodium: 259
For exchange diets, count: 1 1/2 bread/starch, 1 fat

Preparation time: 55 min.

DATE NUT BREAD
YIELD: 16 SLICES

★ ★ ★

8 oz. dates, chopped
1/2 c. chopped walnuts
1 c. raisins
1 tsp. baking soda
1 c. boiling water
2 c. flour
3/4 c. sugar
1 tsp. baking powder
1 egg or 1/4 c. liquid egg
    substitute

Preheat oven to 350° F. Spray 1 loaf pan with nonstick cooking spray. Combine dates, nuts, and raisins in a bowl. Sprinkle baking soda over this and then pour boiling water over the mixture and cover. Set aside. In a mixing bowl, use a pastry cutter to combine flour, sugar, baking powder, and egg or substitute. Add date and liquid mixture and blend well. Pour into prepared loaf pan. Bake for 50 to 60 minutes.

Calories per 1 slice serving: 168
Fat: 3 gm. Cholesterol: 16 mg. with egg
Sodium: 71 mg.
For exchange diets, count: 1 fruit, 1 bread/starch, 1/2 fat

Preparation time: 60 min.

FANCY APPLESAUCE BRAN MUFFINS
YIELD: 24 MUFFINS

★ ★ ★

3 c. All Bran® cereal

2 c. skim milk

1 c. unsweetened applesauce

2 eggs or 1/2 c. liquid egg
    substitute

1/3 c. vegetable oil

2 1/2 c. flour

4 tsp. baking powder

1/2 tsp. salt

3/4 c. brown sugar

1 TB. cinnamon

1 tsp. grated lemon peel

Topping:

1/4 c. brown sugar

2 TB. margarine

Preheat oven to 375° F. In large mixing bowl, combine cereal, milk, and applesauce and allow to sit 10 minutes. Beat in eggs and oil. In separate bowl, stir together all remaining dry ingredients. Fold dry ingredients into cereal mixture, just until moistened. Spoon into 24 muffin tins sprayed with nonstick cooking spray. Combine margarine and sugar for topping and sprinkle on top of muffins. Bake at 375° F. for 15 to 18 minutes.

Calories per muffin: 154
Fat: 5 gm. Cholesterol: 23 mg.
Sodium: 175 mg.
For exchange diets, count: 1/2 fruit,
1 bread/starch, 1 fat

Preparation time: 40 min.

240

HERBED CORN BREAD
YIELD: 8 SQUARES

★ ★ ★

> 1 8 1/2-oz. box corn bread mix
> 1/4 c. nonfat cottage cheese
> 2 TB. dried parsley
> 2 TB. dried chopped chives
> 1 tsp. sage

Preheat oven to 350° F. Prepare mix according to package directions. Stir in cottage cheese, parsley, chives and sage. Pour batter into an 8-inch square pan. Bake for 25 minutes or until lightly browned. Cool and cut into 8 squares. Serve with syrup.

Calories per square: 118
Fat: 3 gm. Cholesterol: 1 mg.
Sodium: 300 mg.
For exchange diets, count: 1 bread/starch,
1 fat

Preparation time: 35 min.

Serving suggestion: Dot each square of hot cornbread with 1 TB. maple syrup or honey.

Calories: 50
Fat: 0 Cholesterol: 0
Sodium: 8 mg.
For exchange diets, count: 1 fruit exchange

POPPY SEED BREAD
YIELD: 2 LOAVES, 18 SLICES EACH

★ ★ ★

My dear neighbor, Diane Tisue, invented this.

> 3 c. flour
> 1/2 tsp. salt
> 1 1/2 tsp. baking powder
> 1 1/2 c. sugar or substitute
> 2 tsp. vanilla
> 1 1/2 c. skim milk
> 3/4 c. vegetable oil
> 1/2 c. frozen orange juice
> concentrate, thawed
> 2 TB. poppy seeds
> 3 eggs or 3/4 c. liquid egg
> substitute
> 1 1/2 tsp. almond extract
> 2 TB. powdered sugar
> 1 TB. finely grated orange
> peel

Preheat oven to 350° F. Put all ingredients except powdered sugar and orange peel into a bowl. Beat for 2 minutes. Divide between 2 loaf pans and bake for 55 minutes. Remove from pan and sprinkle with powdered sugar and grated orange peel while warm.

Calories per 1 slice serving: 125
Fat: 5 gm. Cholesterol: 22 mg. with egg
Sodium: 31 mg.
For exchange diets, count: 1 bread/starch, 1 fat

Preparation time: 60 min.

COLD SWEET 'N SOUR VEGETABLES
YIELD: 8 3/4-C. SERVINGS

★ ★ ★

2 c. celery, chopped very fine
1 large onion, chopped fine
1 20-oz. pkg. frozen mixed
 vegetables, thawed and
 drained

Dressing:
3/4 c. sugar or equivalent in
 substitute
1/2 c. vinegar
1 TB. flour
1 TB. prepared mustard

Combine celery, onion, and drained vegetables in a 2-qt. bowl.
Combine sugar, vinegar, flour, and mustard in a small saucepan.
Bring to a boil and boil for 1 minute. Cool for 10 minutes. Pour
over the vegetables and chill. This salad keeps very well in the
refrigerator for up to 1 week.

Calories per 3/4-c. serving: 132 with sugar, 60 with substitute
Fat: 1 gm. Cholesterol: 0
Sodium: 31 mg.
For exchange diets, count: 2 vegetable, 1 fruit
If using sugar substitute, count just 2 vegetable.

Preparation time: 45 min.

IMPORTANT: If using Equal® brand sugar substitute, do not
cook; add to the cooled dressing.

CRANBERRY SALAD
YIELD: 8 1/2-C. SERVINGS

★ ★ ★

1 3-oz. pkg. sugar-free
  raspberry gelatin
1 3-oz. pkg. sugar-free lemon
  gelatin
1 1/4 c. boiling water
1 c. chopped cranberries
1/2 c. sugar-free lemon lime
  soft drink (7-Up, Sprite,
  Squirt, or Slice are good
  choices)
1 TB. grated lemon peel
1 c. finely chopped apples
1 c. finely chopped celery

Prepare cranberries, apples, and celery. In a 2-qt. mixing bowl,
dissolve gelatin in boiling water. Stir in all remaining
ingredients and chill in 6-c. mold or 1 1/2-qt. pan until firm. Cut
and serve on a bed of greens.

Calories per 1/2-c. serving: 28
Fat: 0 Cholesterol; 0
Sodium: 50 mg.
For exchange diets, count: 1/2 fruit

Preparation time: 2 hours for gelatin to set.

Speed Alert: This gelatin salad requires 2 hr.

CREAMY GARLIC SALAD DRESSING
YIELD: 1 1/2-C. TOTAL OR 12 2-TB. SERVINGS

★ ★ ★

1 c. lite mayonnaise or salad
   dressing
1 TB. instant minced garlic or
   1 1/2 tsp. garlic powder
2 TB. Dijon-style mustard
1/4 c. sugar or equivalent in
   sugar substitute
1/2 tsp. dill seed

Combine all ingredients in blender and process until smooth.
This will keep in the refrigerator for 2 weeks.

Calories per 2-TB. serving: 75 with sugar; 60 with sugar substitute
Fat: 5 gm. Cholesterol: 7 mg.
Sodium: 126 mg.
For exchange diets, count: 1 fat

Preparation time: 10 min.

CRUNCHY BROCCOLI SALAD
YIELD: 8 1-C. SERVINGS

★ ★ ★

1 lg. bunch of fresh broccoli,
chopped into bite-sized
pieces

1 small red onion, sliced thin

4 strips bacon, broiled crisp
and crumbled

1/2 c. raisins

1/2 c. chopped walnuts

Dressing:

1/3 c. light mayonnaise

1/2 c. plain nonfat yogurt

1/4 c. sugar or substitute

2 TB. vinegar

Mix together broccoli, onion, bacon, raisins, and walnuts in a
salad bowl. These ingredients will keep covered in the
refrigerator for 4 days. Combine ingredients for dressing in
shaker container. Pour over broccoli just before serving. Toss
and serve.

Calories per 1-c. serving: 178 with sugar; 154 with sugar substitute
Fat: 4 gm. Cholesterol: 14 mg.
Sodium: 135 mg.
For exchange diets, count: 3 vegetables, 1/2 bread/starch, 1 1/2 fat
With sugar substitute, count: 3 vegetables, 1 1/2 fat

Preparation time: 15 min.

TANGY CABBAGE AND DRIED FRUIT SALAD
YIELD: 8 3/4-C. SERVINGS

★ ★ ★

1/4 c. light mayonnaise
1/4 c. skim milk
2 tsp. lemon juice
1/8 tsp. salt
1/8 tsp. pepper
4 c. shredded cabbage
20 dates, cut unto pieces
1 oz. toasted slivered almonds

In salad bowl, blend mayonnaise, milk, lemon juice, salt, and pepper. Add cabbage and dates, tossing. Chill for 20 minutes. Sprinkle with almonds and serve.

Calories per 3/4-c. serving: 131
Fat: 7 gm. Cholesterol: 2 mg.
Sodium: 74 mg.
For exchange diets, count: 1 vegetable, 1 fruit, 1 fat

Preparation time: 30 min.

HALLOWEEN SALAD
YIELD: 4 3/4-C. SERVINGS

★ ★ ★

> 2 c. shredded carrots
> 1 small can mandarin
>   oranges, drained
> 1/4 c. raisins
> 1 c. nonfat plain yogurt
> 2 TB. light mayonnaise
> 1 TB. lemon juice
> 2 TB. brown sugar or
>   substitute
> 1 tsp. cinnamon
> 2 TB. chopped walnuts

Combine carrots, oranges, and raisins in salad bowl. In small mixing bowl, combine all remaining ingredients, except walnuts, for dressing. Stir to mix, then pour dressing over carrots. Sprinkle walnuts on top before serving.

Calories per 3/4-c. serving: 112
Fat: 4 gm. Cholesterol: 1 mg.
Sodium: 53 mg.
For exchange diets, count: 1 bread/starch, 1 fat

Preparation time: 15 min.

ITALIAN GARDEN SALAD
YIELD: 8 2-C. SERVINGS

★ ★ ★

1 small head cauliflower, cut
  in pieces
1/2 lb. broccoli, cut in pieces
2 ribs celery, cut into 1/4-inch
  slices
1/2 lb. sliced mushrooms
1/2 red onion, sliced thin
1 green pepper, chopped fine
2 carrots, shredded

Dressing:
1/4 c.vegetable oil
1/2 c. lemon juice
1/3 c. Parmesan cheese
1 tsp. oregano
1/4 tsp. garlic powder
1 tsp. basil
1/4 tsp. salt, optional
1/2 tsp. sugar

Layer the vegetables in a 9 x 13-inch pan. Combine ingredients
for dressing in a shaker container and pour over vegetables. The
salad is best if allowed to marinate for at least 1 hour. This keeps
well, covered and refrigerated for 3 days.

Calories per 2-c. serving: 125
Fat: 9 gm. Cholesterol: 5 mg.
Sodium: 204 mg. with salt, 143 mg. without salt
For exchange diets, count: 2 vegetables, 2 fat

Preparation time: 30 min. minimum

SWEET AND SOUR CUCUMBERS
YIELD: 4 1-C. SERVINGS

★ ★ ★

1 medium onion, peeled and
  chopped
4 medium cucumbers, sliced
  thin
1/2 c. sugar or equivalent in
  sugar substitute
1/3 c. vinegar
1/4 tsp. garlic powder
1/8 tsp. celery seed
Dash salt

Wash cucumbers and remove ends. Combine the last 5
ingredients in a salad bowl. Stir to mix. Slice onions and
cucumbers and add to dressing. Toss and serve. This keeps well
refrigerated for 3 days. Serve with a slotted spoon.

Calories per 1-c. serving: 40 with sugar
With sugar substitute: 24
Fat: 0   Cholesterol: 0
Sodium: 231 mg.
For exchange diets, count: 1 vegetable

Preparation time: 15 min.

TAILGATE SALAD
YIELD: 8 3/4-C. SERVINGS

* * *

1 c. frozen cut green beans
4 large potatoes, peeled
3/4 c. feta cheese
1/4 c. sliced olives
1/3 c. sliced red onion
1/4 c. chopped green pepper
3/4 c. sliced radishes

Dressing:
3 TB. vegetable oil
2 tsp. basil
1 tsp. tarragon
2 TB. white wine vinegar
2 tsp. lemon juice
1/4 tsp. garlic powder
1/8 tsp. cayenne (optional)
1/4 tsp. salt (optional)

In a 3-qt. saucepan, cook potatoes in boiling water for 20 minutes. Add frozen beans, cooking 5 minutes more. Drain and cool. Chop the potatoes into 1/2-inch cubes. In a large salad bowl, combine cubed potatoes, beans, cheese, olives, onion, and pepper. Combine ingredients for dressing in a shaker container and pour over salad, tossing to mix. Chill for 1/2 hour before serving. Add radishes just before serving. This keeps well for up to 3 days.

Calories per 3/4-c. serving: 200
Fat: 8 gm. Cholesterol: 6 mg.
Sodium : 185 mg with salt; 124 mg. without salt
For exchange diets, count: 2 bread/starch, 1 1/2 fat

Preparation time: 60 min.

ALMOND CHICKEN WITH VEGETABLES
YIELD: 4 4-OZ. SERVINGS

★ ★ ★

2 chicken breasts, boned and skinned
1 TB. cornstarch
2 TB. sherry
1/2 c. diced sweet red pepper
1/2 c. green onions, sliced
1/4 c. sliced water chestnuts
2 TB. vegetable oil
1 8-oz. can pineapple chunks in juice
　　(drain and reserve juice)
3 TB. slivered almonds

Sauce:
1 1/2 TB. sherry
1 tsp. sesame or vegetable oil
1 tsp. sugar
1/4 c. low-sodium chicken broth
1 1/2 TB. sodium-reduced soy sauce
1 tsp. cornstarch
1 tsp. reserved pineapple juice

Cube chicken. Mix 1 tablespoon cornstarch and 2 tablespoons sherry together and pour over chicken. Set aside. Heat oil in wok or heavy skillet. Add chicken and stir-fry until lightly browned. Add pepper, onion, and water chestnuts. Stir-fry 2 minutes. Meanwhile, combine ingredients for the sauce in a measuring cup or bowl. Add pineapple, slivered almonds, and sauce mixture to the pan. Cook 2 more minutes or until sauce is thickened and smooth.

Calories per 1 1/2-c. serving: 326
Fat: 13 gm. Cholesterol: 67 mg.
Sodium: 299 mg.
For exchange diets, count: 3 lean meat, 1 fat, 1 fruit, 2 vegetable

Preparation time: 15 min.

252

CHICKEN AND ZUCCHINI CREOLE
YIELD: 4 SERVINGS

★ ★ ★

1 lb. chicken pieces
1 c. chopped onion
1/4 tsp. garlic powder
3/4 c. chopped green pepper
2 TB. margarine
2 lb. zucchini, sliced
4 tomatoes
1/4 tsp. salt, optional
1/4 tsp. black pepper
1/4 c. fresh parsley
1/4 c. Parmesan cheese

Melt margarine in a no-stick skillet and saute raw chicken with onion, garlic powder, and green pepper until tender. Stir in zucchini, tomatoes, optional salt, pepper, and parsley. Cook 10 minutes or until zucchini is tender crisp. Sprinkle with Parmesan and serve. This may be prepared and frozen for later use.

Calories per 1 1/2-c. serving: 279
Fat: 10 gm. Cholesterol: 69 mg.
Sodium: 314 mg. with salt; 192 mg. without salt
For exchange diets, count: 4 lean meat, 2 vegetable

Preparation time: 20 min.

CHICKEN BREAST MIDWEST
YIELD: 4 1 1/2-c. SERVINGS

* * *

1 c. apple juice
1 TB. vegetable oil
1 TB. brown sugar
1 TB. light soy sauce
3 TB. lemon juice
2 tsp. dried parsely
1/4 tsp. garlic powder
1/4 tsp. peppercorns
1 tsp. Worcestershire sauce
1 bay leaf
4 skinless chicken breasts
1 TB. vegetable oil
2 c. julienned carrots
2 c. julienned zucchini
2 c. julienned yellow squash

In a small mixing bowl, prepare a marinade of apple juice, oil, brown sugar, soy sauce, lemon juice, parsley, garlic, peppercorns, Worcestershire sauce, and bay leaf. Place chicken breasts in marinade, cover with plastic wrap and refrigerate at least 30 minutes. Remove chicken from bowl and broil for 14 to 18 minutes turning once. Meanwhile, steam the carrots, zucchini and squash with 1 TB. oil and 2 TB. of leftover marinade in a covered dish for 4 to 6 minutes in the MICROWAVE. Arrange the steamed vegetables on a serving platter and place the broiled chicken breasts on top.

Calories per 1 1/2-c. serving : 395
Fat: 12 gm.   Cholesterol: 96 mg.
Sodium: 404 mg.
For exchange diets, count: 4 lean meat, 2 bread/starch, 1 vegetable

Preparation time: 60 min.

CHICKEN CACCIATORE
YIELD: 4 1-C. SERVINGS

★ ★ ★

1 lb. skinned, boned chicken,
 cut into strips

1/2 c. chopped onion

1 medium green pepper, cut
 into strips

1 TB. vegetable oil

16 oz. no added salt whole
 tomatoes

8 oz. no added salt tomato
 sauce

1/2 tsp. oregano

1/2 tsp. basil

1 c. quick rice

Saute chicken, onion, and pepper in oil. Stir in tomatoes, sauce,
and seasonings and bring to a boil. Stir in rice. Cover. Reduce
heat to low. Cook for 10 minutes. This may be prepared and
frozen for later use. Defrost 10 minutes in microwave, then heat
10 to 15 minutes on high power.

Calories per 1-c. serving: 339
Fat: 6 gm. Cholesterol: 68 mg.
Sodium: 104 mg.
For exchange diets, count: 3 lean meat, 2 bread/starch, 2 vegetable

Preparation time: 20 min.

CHICKEN STROGANOFF
YIELD: 4 4-OZ. SERVINGS

★ ★ ★

2 whole chicken breasts, split,
   boned, and skinned
1/4 tsp. garlic powder
1/4 tsp. white pepper
1/2 c. Campbell's Special
   Request® Cream of
   Mushroom Soup
1 c. plain yogurt
6-oz. can sliced mushrooms,
   drained
2 TB. sherry
1/4 c. Parmesan cheese

Preheat oven to 350° F. Spray an 8 x 11-inch casserole dish with nonstick cooking spray. Place chicken breasts in casserole. Do not overlap. Sprinkle with garlic and pepper. Combine soup, yogurt, and mushrooms and pour over chicken. Sprinkle cheese over all. Bake for 50 minutes or MICROWAVE, covered on high power for 18 minutes or until chicken is tender. Serve with your favorite cooked noodles.

Calories per 4 oz. of Stroganoff and 1/2 chicken breast
(not including noodles): 202
Fat: 6 gm. Cholesterol: 63 mg.
Sodium: 133 mg.
For exchange diets, count: 3 lean meat, 1/2 skim milk

Preparation time: 30 min.

FISH AND POTATO BAKE
YIELD: 4 1 1/2-C. SERVINGS

★ ★ ★

1 onion, chopped

2 green peppers, cut in 1/2-inch strips

1/4 tsp. garlic powder

1 TB. vegetable oil

1 15-oz. can Italian style stewed tomatoes

1/4 tsp. pepper

1 16-oz. can new potatoes, drained and sliced

1 lb. white fish fillets, cut into chunks

Preheat oven to 375° F. (Recipe can be microwaved.) Saute onion, green pepper, and garlic powder in oil in a skillet for 5 minutes. Pour in tomatoes, cover, and simmer for 5 minutes. Spread 3 TB. of sauce over bottom of 8-inch square casserole dish. Layer with potatoes and fish, then pour remaining sauce over the top. Bake for 25 minutes or until fish is flaky, or MICROWAVE on high power for 12 to 14 minutes.

Calories per serving: 240
Fat: 6 gm. Cholesterol: 77 mg.
Sodium: 263 mg.
For exchange diets, count: 3 lean meat, 1 bread/starch

Preparation time: 25 min. using microwave method

JAMBALAYA
YIELD: 8 1 1/2-C. SERVINGS

★ ★ ★

2 TB. oil
1 large green pepper, diced
2 medium onions, chopped
1/2 tsp. garlic powder
1/2 c. cubed cooked lean ham
2 c. quick type rice
2 1-lb., 12-oz. cans no added
    salt tomatoes
1 tsp. hot pepper sauce
1 1/2 lb. peeled and deveined
    shrimp
(For economy meal,
    substitute chunks of white
    fish, such as cod or
    haddock.)
1/2 tsp. pepper
1 tsp. basil
1/2 tsp. thyme

In 4-qt. Dutch oven, heat oil. Saute pepper, onion, and garlic. Add ham and brown. Stir in all remaining ingredients except for shrimp. Simmer for 20 minutes. Add shrimp or white fish and cook for 5 minutes or until shrimp is pink or white fish is tender and flaky. This can be prepared and frozen for later use. Defrost for 10 minutes in MICROWAVE. Then cook on high power for 10 to 15 minutes.

Calories per 1 1/2-c. serving: 292
Fat: 5 gm. Cholesterol: 136 mg.
Sodium: 209 mg.
For exchange diets, count: 1 1/2 bread/starch, 2 vegetable, 2 lean meat

Preparation time: 35 min.

PINEAPPLE CHICKEN
YIELD: 4 4-OZ. SERVINGS

★ ★ ★

1/3 c. diet Italian salad
  dressing
1 20-oz. can crushed
  pineapple, drained, with
  liquid reserved
2 TB. brown sugar
1/2 tsp. ginger
4 chicken breasts, skinned,
  boned, and pounded
1/3 c. chopped green pepper
1/4 c. slivered almonds
1 TB. cornstarch

Marinate chicken breasts in pineapple juice, brown sugar, and ginger in the refrigerator overnight (8 to 24 hours; or 30 minutes minimum). Preheat oven to 375° F. In small bowl, combine crushed pineapple, pepper, and almonds. Remove chicken from marinade and spoon pineapple mixture evenly on top of breasts. Roll them up, secure with a toothpick, and place seam side down in a baking dish sprayed with nonstick cooking spray. Pour 1/4 c. of marinade over the chicken. Cover and bake for 35 minutes or MICROWAVE on 70% power for 14 minutes until chicken is tender. Remove chicken to platter. In small pan, combine remaining marinade and chicken dish drippings with cornstarch and cook for 2 minutes until thick. Pour over chicken.

Calories per 4-oz. serving: 276
Fat: 8 gm. Cholesterol: 690 mg.
Sodium: 183 mg.
For exchange diets, count: 3 lean meat, 1 bread/starch, 1 fruit

Preparation time: 55 min., plus 30 min. minimum for marinating

PHEASANT CASSEROLE
YIELD: 4 4-OZ. SERVINGS

★ ★ ★

1 small box Uncle Ben's
   Brown and Wild Rice®

2 c. chopped cooked pheasant

1/3 c. chopped water
   chestnuts

1/3 c. Mary's Cream Soup
   Substitute (see page 208)

1 small can mushrooms, well
   drained

1 3/4 c. water

Steam or boil pheasant until tender. Cool and remove meat from the bone, chopping into bite-sized pieces. Cook the rice according to package directions. While the rice is cooking, preheat oven to 350° F. Spray a 2-qt. casserole dish with nonstick cooking spray. Mix 1/3 c. Mary's Cream Soup Substitute with 1 3/4 c. water. Transfer cooked rice, meat, water chestnuts, drained mushrooms, and soup and water mixture to the dish and stir. Bake uncovered for 30 minutes.

Calories per 1/4 recipe: 294
Fat: 4 gm. Cholesterol: 39 mg.
Sodium: 397 mg.
For exchange diets count: 3 lean meat, 1 vegetable, 1 1/2 bread/starch

Preparation time: 45 minutes, if pheasant is pre-cooked.

ROAST VENISON IN THE CROCKPOT
YIELD: 8 4-OZ. SERVINGS

★ ★ ★

2 lb. venison
2 TB. flour
1 TB oil
1/2 tsp. garlic powder
1 large onion, sliced
2 TB. brown sugar
1 tsp. mustard
1 TB. Worcestershire sauce
1/4 c. lemon juice
1 16-oz. can no added salt
   tomatoes

Marinade:
1/2 c. vinegar
1/2 tsp. garlic powder
2 TB. salt
Cold water to cover meat

Mix vinegar, garlic powder, and salt together. Place meat in a deep flat pan. Pour cold water over meat and add vinegar mixture. Marinate overnight. Remove from marinade and drain well. Roll meat in flour and brown in 1 TB. vegetable oil in a skillet. Transfer browned meat to the crockpot. Add all remaining ingredients and cook on low for 8 hours. This makes an excellent leftover.

Calories per 4-oz. serving: 291
Fat: 10 gm. Cholesterol: 65 mg.
Sodium: 86 mg.
For exchange diets, count: 3 lean meat, 1 1/2 bread/starch

Preparation time: Overnight marinade, then 8 hours in crockpot.

Speed Alert: For best results with venison, marinate overnight.

261

ROMANTIC CHICKEN MARSALA
YIELD: 4 8-OZ. SERVINGS

★ ★ ★

> 1 TB. liquid oil margarine
> 1/4 c. chopped onion
> 1/2 c. chopped celery
> 1 c. sliced mushrooms
> 1 lb. skinless chicken pieces
> 1/4 tsp. sage
> 1/2 c. white wine
> 1 c. skim milk
> 1 TB. flour
> 1/4 tsp. white pepper
> 1/4 tsp. salt, optional

In saucepan, saute onion, celery, and mushrooms in margarine until tender. Add chicken and sage, cooking for 5 more minutes. Pour in wine and cook for 5 more minutes, allowing liquid to evaporate. In shaker container, combine flour and milk. Slowly stir into sauce, cooking 3 minutes or until thick. Stir in salt and pepper. Serve over tender cooked thick noodles.

Calories per 1-c. serving of chicken (noodles not included): 219
Fat: 7 gm. Cholesterol: 80 mg.
Sodium: 299 mg. with salt; 177 mg. without salt
For exchange diets, count: 3 lean meat, 2 vegetable

Preparation time: 20 min.

STEAMED FISH FILLETS
YIELD: 4 4-OZ. SERVINGS

★ ★ ★

1 lb. white fish fillets (cod, haddock, orange roughy, bluegill, northern, or trout work well)
1 c. tomato juice
1 tsp. oregano
1/4 tsp. seasoned salt (optional)
1/4 tsp. white pepper

Preheat oven to 400° F. (Fish can be microwaved.) Place fillets in baking dish. Cover with tomato juice and seasonings. Bake, covered, for 12 to 18 minutes, until fish is flaky. To MICROWAVE, cover baking dish and bake on high power for 5 to 8 minutes.

Calories per 4-oz. serving: 94
Fat: 1 gm. Cholesterol: 47 mg.
Sodium: 298 mg. with salt; 176 mg. without salt
For exchange diets, count: 3 lean meat

Preparation time: 15 min.

SEAFOOD SCAMPI
YIELD: 4 1 1/2-C. SERVINGS

★ ★ ★

1 lb. seafood of choice
(shrimp, mock crab, cod)
1 onion, chopped
1/2 tsp. garlic powder
1 TB. liquid oil margarine
8 oz. no salt added chicken
broth
1 tsp. no salt added chicken
bouillon
1 TB. flour
1 red pepper, chopped
1 TB. lemon juice
1/4 tsp. salt, optional
1 1/2 c. quick rice
1/4 c. fresh parsley

Saute seafood, onion, and garlic powder in margarine in large skillet until seafood turns white. Combine broth, bouillon, and flour in a shaker container. Stir into seafood mixture. Add pepper, lemon juice, and optional salt. Bring to a boil. Stir in rice and parsley. Cover. Remove from heat and let stand for 5 minutes. Serve.

Calories per 1 1/2-c. serving: 266
Fat: 4 gm. Cholesterol: 43 mg.
Sodium: 495 mg. with salt, 373 mg. without salt
For exchange diets, count: 2 lean meat, 1 1/2 bread/starch, 1 vegetable

Preparation time: 15 min.

STUFFED SOLE
YIELD: 4 4-OZ. SERVINGS

★ ★ ★

1 c. sliced mushrooms

1/2 c. sliced green onions

1 TB. vegetable oil

3/4 c. oatmeal or bread
crumbs

1 egg or 1/4 c. liquid egg
substitute

1/4 tsp. salt, optional

2 TB. lemon juice

1/2 tsp. marjoram

1 lb. sole, flounder, orange
roughy, or cod fillets

Paprika

Preheat oven to 375° F. Saute mushrooms and onions in oil for 3
minutes. Add oatmeal or bread crumbs, egg, salt, 1 TB. lemon
juice, and marjoram. Divide stuffing mixture among the fillets,
spreading to within 1/2 inch of the edge. Roll up and secure with
a toothpick and place seam side down in an 8-inch square baking
dish. Sprinkle with the other 1 TB. of lemon juice, dust with
paprika, and bake for 20 minutes or MICROWAVE for 8
minutes, just until the fish flakes easily with a fork.

Calories per 4-oz. serving: 260
Fat: 11 gm. Cholesterol: 114 mg. with egg, 50 mg. with substitute
Sodium: 263 mg. with salt, 141 mg. without salt
For exchange diets, count: 3 lean meat, 1 bread/starch

Preparation time: 25 min.

TARRAGON TURKEY
YIELD: 8 TO 10 SERVINGS FROM AN 8-LB. TURKEY

★ ★ ★

Turkeys are best roasted on a rack at 325° F. An 8 to 12 lb.
turkey requires 4 hours; allow for 4 1/2 hours for a 12 to 16 lb.
bird. Cover the turkey loosely with foil for a beautiful browned
appearance. Roast with breast down because the juices keep the
white meat moist. Allow the roasted bird to sit 15 minutes at
room temperature before carving. Serve a 3 to 5 oz. portion of
turkey with this sauce on the side:

Sauce:
Yield: 8 3-TB. servings or
   1 1/2 c.
1 TB. vegetable oil
2 TB. finely diced onion
1/4 c. white wine
2 TB. tarragon wine vinegar
1 c. yogurt
2 TB. Dijon mustard
1/8 tsp. dried tarragon leaves,
   crushed
1/2 tsp. sugar

In a saucepan, heat oil, and saute onion. Stir in white wine and
vinegar and simmer for 3 minutes, reducing volume. Lower heat
and fold in yogurt, mustard, tarragon, and sugar. Keep sauce
warm on low heat or prepare ahead of time and chill. MICRO-
WAVE the sauce in a glass pitcher for 1 1/2 minutes just before
serving.

Calories per 3 TB. of sauce: 32
Fat: 2 gm. Cholesterol: less than 1 mg.
Sodium: 87 mg.
For exchange diets, count: 1/2 skim milk

Preparation time: 10 min. for sauce

LEFTOVER TURKEY, KABOB STYLE
YIELD: 4 SERVINGS

★ ★ ★

4 medium yams or sweet
   potatoes
8 oz. pineapple chunks, in
   juice
1 tsp. cornstarch
1/2 tsp. cinnamon
1/4 tsp. dry mustard
1/8 tsp. ground cloves
1/2 c. jellied cranberry sauce
3/4 lb. roast turkey, cut into
   chunks
4 small canned onions

Cut off woody stem of yams. Place in a covered microwave-proof
baking dish with 2 TB. water. MICROWAVE for 10 minutes on
high power until tender. Cool the yams long enough to be able to
peel and quarter them. Meanwhile, drain pineapple, and
combine juice in small saucepan with cornstarch, cinnamon,
mustard, cloves, and cranberry sauce. Heat until thick and
bubbly. On 4 skewers, thread turkey, yam, pineapple chunks,
and onions. Broil for 8 minutes, brushing with sauce on both
sides during broiling. Pass remaining sauce at the table.

Calories per serving: 393
Fat: 6 gm. Cholesterol: 70 mg.
Sodium: 195 mg.
For exchange diets, count: 2 1/2 bread/starch, 1 fat, 3 lean meat

Preparation time: 30 min.

TURKEY WITH ORANGE RAISIN SAUCE
YIELD: 8 1/3-C. SERVINGS (FOR A 10 LB. TURKEY)

★ ★ ★

3 TB. margarine
1/4 c. minced onion
1/2 c. raisins
1/2 c. orange juice
1/4 c. honey
1 TB. grated orange peel
1/2 c. water

Prepare and start a 10 to 12 lb. turkey roasting. See page 266 for directions on roasting turkeys. To prepare sauce, melt margarine in a small saucepan. Add onion and saute until tender. Stir in raisins, orange juice, honey, and orange peeling. Using a wire whisk, stir in cornstarch and water. Cook over medium heat just until boiling, then reduce heat and cook for 3 more minutes. Pour sauce over turkey 1/2 hour before it is done, leaving the bird uncovered to promote a brown glazing.

Calories per 1/3-c. of sauce: 155
Fat: 6 gm. Cholesterol: 0
Sodium: 27 mg.
For exchange diets, count: 1 1/2 fruit, and 1 fat for 1/3 c. of sauce

Calories per 3-oz. serving of turkey: 165
Fat: 9 gm. Cholesterol: 51 mg.
Sodium: 63 mg.
For exchange diets, count: 3 oz. of turkey as 3 lean meat

Preparation time: 10 min. for sauce

Speed Alert: Preparation time depends on size of turkey.

APPLE GLAZED PORK KABOBS
YIELD: 4 4-OZ. SERVINGS

★ ★ ★

1 lb. boneless pork loin, cut
    into 1-inch cubes
2 TB. lemon juice
1/4 tsp. salt (optional)

Apple Glaze:
1/3 c. apple jelly
1 TB. lemon juice
1/8 tsp. cinnamon
1 TB. margarine

Trim pork and cube. Sprinkle lemon juice and salt over pork in a
shallow pan. In a glass measuring cup, mix jelly, lemon juice,
cinnamon, and melted margarine. Thread pork cubes onto
skewers and baste with glaze. Grill or broil kabobs 10 to 12
minutes, turning and basting 2 more times.

Calories per 4-oz. serving: 310
Fat: 12 gm. Cholesterol: 92 mg.
Sodium: 214 mg. with salt; 146 mg. without salt
For exchange diets, count: 4 lean meat, 1 bread/starch

Preparation time: 30 min.

BRUSHED BEEF ROAST
YIELD: 8 4-OZ. SLICES

★ ★ ★

> 1/4 c. liquid oil margarine
> 2 TB. red wine
> 1/4 c. minced onion
> 2 TB. lemon juice
> 1/2 tsp. oregano
> 1/4 tsp. marjoram
> 1/4 tsp. thyme
> 1/4 tsp. pepper
> 1/4 tsp. garlic powder
> 2 lb. flank steak, 2 inches
>   thick

Melt margarine and mix in wine, onion, lemon juice, and spices.
Put this marinade in a plastic bag with flank steak. Seal. Turn
the bag to coat the meat, and let stand for at least 30 minutes.
Remove the meat from the bag and place on a broiling pan or
rack. Brush the surface of the meat with marinade and broil for
6 minutes. Turn and brush other side of steak with remaining
marinade. Broil 8 more minutes. Slice and serve.

Calories per 4-oz. slice: 205
Fat: 11 gm. Cholesterol: 72 mg.
Sodium: 84 mg.
For exchange diets, count: 4 lean meat

Preparation time: 50 min.

CHINESE PORK AND BROCCOLI
YIELD: 6 1-C. SERVINGS

★ ★ ★

1 bunch fresh broccoli
1 lb. pork loin or shoulder
2 tsp. cornstarch
1/2 tsp. sugar
1 TB. soy sauce
2 TB. water
2 TB. vegetable oil
4 green onions, diagonally
   sliced
1 tsp. ginger
1/2 tsp. dried crushed hot
   peppers (optional)
2 TB. teriyaki sauce
1 TB. cornstarch
1/2 c. no added salt chicken
   broth
1/4 c. water

Wash and cut broccoli into bite-sized pieces. Trim fat from pork
and cut meat into 1 x 1 1/2-inch strips. Mix corn starch, sugar,
soy sauce, and water together in a small bowl. Add pork and toss
to coat. In wok or large skillet, heat oil and add pork and
marinade. Brown meat to near done. Transfer browned meat
back to the bowl. Heat remaining oil in skillet and saute green
onions, ginger, and hot peppers for 2 minutes. Add broccoli and
cook for 8 to10 minutes. In a glass measuring cup, whisk
together teriyaki sauce, ginger, broth, and water. Add to skillet
and cook until thick. Add cooked pork and heat through. Serve
over rice.

Calories per 1-c. serving pork and broccoli (rice not included): 219
Fat: 11 gm. Cholesterol: 72 mg.
Sodium: 392 mg.
For exchange diets, count: 3 lean meat, 1 vegetable

Preparation time: 35 min.

IOWA BEEF STROGANOFF
YIELD: 6 SERVINGS

★ ★ ★

1 lb. beef top round	3 c. low-sodium beef broth
1/4 tsp. freshly ground black pepper	2 TB. no salt added tomato paste
4 oz. fresh mushrooms, sliced thin	1 tsp. dry mustard
1 onion, sliced	1/4 tsp. oregano
2 TB. oil	1/4 tsp. dill weed
3 TB. flour	1 Tb. sherry
	1/3 c. low-fat yogurt

Remove all visible fat from meat and cut into thin strips, about 2 inches long. Sprinkle with pepper. In a heavy skillet, saute mushrooms in oil until tender. Remove from skillet, and saute onions in the same oil until brown. Remove from skillet. Brown meat quickly in skillet, remove, and set aside. Blend the flour into the oil in the skillet and gradually add the broth, stirring constantly until smooth and thick. Add the tomato paste, mustard, oregano, dill weed, and sherry. Blend well. Combine the sauce with the meat, mushrooms, and onions in skillet. Simmer for 20 minutes, stirring occasionally. Blend in the yogurt just before serving. Serve with rice or noodles.

Calories per 1-c. serving (not including rice): 197
Fat: 8 gm. Cholesterol: 49 mg.
Sodium: 56 mg.
For exchange diets, count: 3 lean meat, 1 vegetable

Preparation time: 35 min.

LONDON BROIL
YIELD: 4 3-OZ. SERVINGS

★ ★ ★

1 envelope Italian salad dressing mix
1/4 c. red wine
2 TB. vegetable oil
1 lb. flank steak

Score flank steak 1/8-inch deep in criss-cross pattern on both sides. Combine the dressing mix with the wine and oil in a shaker container. Pour over the meat in a shallow pan and marinate, covered, in the refrigerator overnight (or 8 hours). Broil or grill the meat to desired doneness and discard remaining marinade.

Calories per 3-oz. serving: 194
Fat: 10 gm. Cholesterol: 69 mg.
Sodium: 233 mg.
For exchange diets, count: 3 lean meat

Preparation time: 8 hours for marinade

Speed Alert: Flank steak requires an 8-hour marinade.

MARINATED LOIN OF PORK
YIELD: 8 4-OZ. SERVINGS

★ ★ ★

> 2 lb. pork loin, trimmed
> 1 can light beer
> 1/2 c. apple juice
> 1 tsp. thyme
> 1 TB. brown sugar
> 1/2 tsp. black pepper

Preheat oven to 400° F. Combine ingredients for marinade in a shaker container. Pour over the pork loin in a shallow pan. Cover. Refrigerate for at least 30 minutes. Drain marinade and save. Roast meat at 400° F. for 20 minutes. Reduce heat to 325° F. and continue roasting for 1 1/2 hours. Pour some reserved marinade over the meat at 30 minute intervals. Meat is well done when thermometer registers 170° F. Allow meat to cool for 20 minutes. Slice and serve.

Calories per 4-oz. serving: 197
Fat: 7 gm. Cholesterol: 54 mg.
Sodium: 47 mg.
For exchange diets, count: 3 lean meat, 1/2 fruit

Preparation time: 2 hours for marinade and roast.

Speed Alert: Pork roast requires 1 1/2 hours to reach 170° F.

MICROWAVE MEATLOAF
YIELD: 4 4-OZ. SERVINGS

★ ★ ★

1 egg or 1/4 c. liquid egg
    substitute
1/4 c. skim milk
1/4 c. oat bran or oatmeal
1/4 c. chopped onion
1/4 tsp. salt (optional)
1/2 tsp. pepper
1 lb. lean ground beef
Glaze:
1/4 c. no added salt tomato
    sauce
1 TB. brown sugar
1/2 tsp. yellow mustard
1/4 tsp. thyme

Combine ingredients for loaf in a 1-qt. mixing bowl. Pat into microwave-safe loaf pan. Cook, covered, for 14 minutes on high power. Drain well. Combine ingredients for glaze. Spread over the loaf. Cook on high power for 5 minutes. Let stand for 5 more minutes, slice, and serve.

Calories per 4-oz. serving: 273
Fat: 12 gm. Cholesterol: 95 mg. with egg; 30 mg. with substitute
Sodium: 211 mg. with salt; 89 mg. without salt
For exchange diets, count: 4 lean meat, 1 bread/starch

Preparation time: 30 min.

Rouladin

(a German word for Steak Rolls)
Yield: 4 4-oz. servings

* * *

> 4 minute steaks, 4 oz. each
> 2 tsp. Dijon mustard
> 1/2 tsp. salt, optional
> 1 large pickle, cut into four
>   thin strips
> 2 strips bacon, diced fine
> 1 lg. onion, chopped fine
> 1 1/2 c. no added salt beef
>   broth
> 4 peppercorns
> 1 bay leaf
> 1 TB. cornstarch

In a small skillet, cook onion and bacon until bacon is crisp.
Drain well. In the meantime, pound steaks flat, then spread with
mustard and sprinkle with salt. Sprinkle with bacon and onion
mixture and place one strip of pickle down the center of each
steak. Roll the steaks up and secure with a toothpick or string.
Brown the steaks in the skillet. Transfer the steaks to a Dutch
oven. Pour 1 c. broth, peppercorns, and bay leaf over steaks and
cover. Bake for 30 minutes at 350° F. Just before the meat is
done, mix the cornstarch with the remaining 1/2 c. broth. Add it
to the meat juices and stir until thick. Serve as a sauce over the
steak rolls.

Calories per 4-oz. serving: 238
Fat: 12 gm. Cholesterol: 65 mg.
Sodium: 346 mg. with salt; 285 mg. without
For exchange diets, count: 4 lean meat, 1 vegetable

Preparation time: 50 min.

TEX MEX PORKLOAF
YIELD: 4 3-OZ. SERVINGS

★ ★ ★

1 lb. lean ground pork
1/4 c. dried bread crumbs
1/3 c. chopped onion
1/4 c. skim milk
1 1/2 tsp. chili powder
1/2 tsp. cumin
1/2 tsp. oregano
1/4 tsp. garlic powder
1/4 tsp. black pepper
1/8 tsp. salt, optional

Preheat oven to 350° F. Combine pork, crumbs, onion, milk, and seasonings in a large bowl, mixing lightly. Shape into a 6 x 3 x 3-inch loaf. Place loaf on a rack in a shallow roasting pan. Bake for 45 to 55 minutes. Remove from oven and allow to stand for 5 minutes. Slice and serve.

Calories per 3-oz. serving: 244
Fat: 11 gm. Cholesterol: 81 mg.
Sodium: 213 mg. with salt; 152 mg. without salt
For exchange diets, count: 3 lean meat, 1 bread/starch

Preparation time: 60 min.

TRADITIONAL POT ROAST
YIELD: 8 3-OZ. MEAT AND 3/4-C. VEGETABLE SERVINGS

★ ★ ★

2 lb. boneless chuck roast,
   trimmed well
2 c. no added salt beef broth
1/2 c. red wine
1/2 tsp. garlic powder
1/2 c. chopped onion
1 TB. Dijon mustard
2 tsp. Worcestershire sauce
1 tsp. thyme
4 potatoes, peeled and
   quartered
6 medium carrots, peeled and
   chunked

Place chuck roast in a glass dish. Combine broth, wine, garlic, onion, mustard, Worcestershire sauce, and thyme in a shaker and pour over the meat. Cover. Marinate in refrigerator for at least 30 minutes or up to 24 hours. Place meat and marinade in Dutch oven or crock pot. Add potatoes and carrots. Simmer in Dutch oven for 3 hours or cook in crock pot until tender. Marinating tenderizes the chuck. (If you use a tender cut, such as loin, place all ingredients in crock pot and simmer.)

Calories per 9-oz. serving: 261
Fat: 9 gm. Cholesterol: 85 mg.
Sodium: 128 mg.
For exchange diets, count: 3 lean meat, 1/2 bread/starch, 2 vegetable

Preparation time: 3 to 6 hours in crock pot

Speed Alert: This crock pot recipe takes 3 to 6 hours.

APPLE DRESSING
YIELD: 8 1-c. SERVINGS

★ ★ ★

2 c. bread crumbs
4 c. chopped apples
1 small onion, chopped
3 stalks celery, chopped
1/4 c. raisins
1/2 c. apple juice
2 TB. brown sugar
1/4 tsp. salt
1 tsp. cinnamon
2 TB. margarine, melted

Preheat oven to 350° F. Combine crumbs, apple, onion, celery, and raisins in a 3-qt. baking pan that has been sprayed with nonstick cooking spray. In a small mixing bowl, combine remaining ingredients, stirring to blend. Pour liquid over bread mixture and toss to coat. Cover and bake for 35 minutes. Uncover and bake 10 more minutes to promote crusting.

Calories per 1-c. serving: 169
Fat: 1 gm. Cholesterol: 0
Sodium: 265 mg.
For exchange diets, count: 1 fruit, 1 1/2 bread/starch

Preparation time: 60 min.

BAKED CARROTS AND SPROUTS
YIELD: 8 1-C. SERVINGS

★ ★ ★

2 TB. liquid oil margarine
1/2 c. chopped onion
1/4 c. flour
1 tsp. dill weed
3 c. skim milk
1/3 c. chopped fresh parsley
2 c. fresh Brussels sprouts
3 c. sliced fresh carrots

Steam fresh sprouts and carrots with 2 TB. water in a covered dish in the MICROWAVE for 5 minutes. Drain off water. Meanwhile, saute onion in margarine in a medium-sized skillet. Stir in flour and dill weed, then gradually stir in milk. Cook until thick. Pour sauce over vegetables, and top with fresh parsley. MICROWAVE for 12 minutes, uncovered, on high power or bake, uncovered, for 30 minutes at 350° F.

Calories per 1-c. serving: 108
Fat: 4 gm. Cholesterol: 1 mg.
Sodium: 227 mg.
For exchange diets, count: 1/2 bread/starch,
1 vegetable, 1 fat

Preparation time: 20 min. if microwaved

BROCCOLI RICE CASSEROLE
YIELD: 4 1 1/2-C. SERVINGS

★ ★ ★

1/2 c. diced celery
1/2 c. chopped onion
1/2 lb. fresh mushrooms
2 TB. margarine
2 10-oz. pkgs. chopped
   broccoli
1 c. quick rice, uncooked
2 oz. Light American cheese,
   shredded
2/3 c. Mary's Cream Soup
   Substitute, page 208

Preheat oven to 350° F. (Recipe can also be microwaved.) In a no-stick skillet, saute onion, celery, and sliced mushrooms in margarine until tender. Using 1 large or two small casserole dishes, combine sauteed vegetables with broccoli, rice, and shredded cheese. Combine 2/3 c. Cream Soup Substitute with 2 1/2 c. water in a shaker container. Add to the other ingredients and mix well. Bake for 30 minutes or MICROWAVE on high power for 15 to 18 minutes, until mixture is bubbly.

Calories per 1 1/2-c. serving: 132
Fat: 5 gm. Cholesterol: 4 mg.
Sodium: 302 mg.
For exchange diets, count: 1 bread/starch, 1 vegetable, 1 fat

Preparation time: 45 min.

CHRISTMAS STUFFING
YIELD: 12 3/4-C. SERVINGS

* * *

4 c. fresh bread crumbs
1/2 c. skim milk
1 c. no added salt chicken
   broth
1/2 c. diced onion
1 TB. margarine, melted
1/2 lb. turkey sausage,
   browned and drained
3/4 c. chopped celery
1/4 c. raisins
1/4 c. cranberries
1 tsp. sage

Preheat oven to 350° F. Spray a 2-qt. casserole dish with nonstick cooking spray. Combine all ingredients in the 2-qt. casserole. Cover and bake for 35 minutes. Add additional broth if the mixture becomes dry while baking. Remove cover and brown the top for 10 minutes.

Calories per 3/4-c. serving: 177
Fat: 5 gm. Cholesterol: 14 mg.
Sodium: 186 mg.
For exchange diets, count: 1 lean meat, 1/2 fruit, 1 bread/starch, 1/2 fat

Preparation time: 60 min.

FRUIT STUFFING
YIELD: 8 3/4-C. SERVINGS

★ ★ ★

1 c. chopped cranberries

2 TB. sugar

12 slices raisin bread, cut into cubes

1 c. no added salt chicken or turkey broth

2 TB. margarine, melted

2 tsp. grated orange peel

1/8 tsp salt

2 TB. orange juice

Preheat oven to 325° F. Combine all ingredients in a mixing bowl, stirring to moisten bread. Stuff turkey loosely and roast, or stir and transfer to a casserole dish that has been sprayed with nonstick cooking spray. Bake for 35 minutes, removing the cover the last ten minutes to brown.

Calories per 3/4-c. serving: 141
Fat: 4 gm. Cholesterol: 0
Sodium: 203 mg.
For exchange diets, count: 1 bread/starch, 1 fat

Preparation time: 60 min.

GERMAN POTATO SALAD
YIELD: 8 1/2-c. SERVINGS

★ ★ ★

4 large potatoes, boiled,
  peeled, and diced

3 strips bacon, diced, fried
  crisp, and drained well

4 green onions, diced

Dressing:

1/4 tsp. pepper

1 TB. oil

4 TB. vinegar

1 tsp. sugar

1/4 tsp. salt

Combine potatoes, bacon, and onions in a bowl. Use a shaker jar
to combine the dressing ingredients. Just before serving, pour
dressing over the potatoes and toss. Serve at room temperature.
Recipe is for 8 servings. It works well to use half the potato
mixture and half the dressing for 2 meals of 4 servings each.

Calories per 1/2-c. serving: 94
Fat: 3 gm. Cholesterol: 2 mg.
Sodium: 92 mg.
For exchange diets, count: 1 bread/starch, 1/2 fat

Preparation time: 40 min.

GERMAN RED CABBAGE
YIELD: 8 1-C. SERVINGS

★ ★ ★

1 head red cabbage
1 c. water
1/2 c. chopped onion
1 small apple, chopped
3 bay leaves
1/4 c. vinegar
2 TB. brown sugar
4 slices bacon, broiled crisp
    and crumbled

Coarsely shred cabbage and place in 3-qt. saucepan with water, onion, apple, and bay leaves. Bring to a boil and cook for 12 to 15 minutes. Drain in colander, removing bay leaves. Transfer to a serving bowl and add vinegar, sugar, and bacon. Mix well and serve immediately.

Calories per 1-c. serving: 92
Fat: 2 gm. Cholesterol: 3 mg.
Sodium: 70 mg.
For exchange diets, count: 2 vegetable, 1 fat

Preparation time: 20 min.

GREEN BEANS WITH GARLIC DRESSING
YIELD: 4 SERVINGS

★ ★ ★

> 4 c. fresh or fresh frozen
>   green beans
> 1/2 c. reduced-calorie French
>   dressing
> 2 TB. minced onion
> 1/2 tsp. garlic powder
> 1/4 tsp. oregano

Cook beans until tender. Meanwhile, combine dressing, garlic, onion, and oregano in a shaker container. Transfer beans to a serving bowl. Toss beans and dressing. Serve immediately.

Calories per 1-c. serving: 71
Fat: 1 gm. Cholesterol: less than 1 mg.
Sodium: 150 mg.
For exchange diets, count: 3 vegetable

Preparation time: 25 min.

RICE CREOLE
YIELD: 4 1-C. SERVINGS

★ ★ ★

3 c. no added salt tomato juice
1/2 c. quick rice
1/4 tsp. salt (optional)
1/4 tsp. pepper
1/4 c. chopped onion
1/4 c. celery
2 slices bacon, broiled crisp
    and crumbled

Combine all ingredients in a 2-qt. baking dish. MICROWAVE for 20 minutes on medium power until the mixture has thickened. Serve in bowls as a side dish. May simmer uncovered on stove top for 35 minutes, instead of using microwave method.

Calories per 1-c. serving: 125
Fat: 2 gm. Cholesterol: 3 mg.
Sodium: 180 mg. with salt; 58 mg. without salt
For exchange diets, count: 1 vegetable, 1 bread/starch

Preparation time: 30 min.

ANITA'S PRETTY FRUIT CUPS
YIELD: 4 1-C. SERVINGS

★ ★ ★

This recipe comes from a cook for all seasons, Anita Schmelzer.

> 1 c. boiling water
> 3 oz. reduced-calorie lemon
>   gelatin
> 3 oz. frozen orange juice
>   concentrate
> 1 medium banana, sliced
> 1/2 c. mandarin orange slices
> 1/2 c. crushed pineapple

Boil water and pour over gelatin in a medium bowl. Stir to
dissolve. Add 3 oz. frozen orange juice concentrate. Stir to mix,
then refrigerate for 1/2 hour until partially set. Fold in bananas,
oranges, and pineapple. Pour into 4 tall glass dessert dishes.
Chill until set.

Calories per serving: 105
Fat: 0 Cholesterol: 0
Sodium: 3 mg.
For exchange diets, count: 2 fruit

Preparation time: 2 hours

Speed Alert: This recipe requires 2 hours for gelatin to set.

CHOCOLATE MOUSSE IN THE BLENDER
YIELD: 4 1/2-C. SERVINGS

★ ★ ★

1 egg
1 envelope unflavored gelatin
4 TB. cold water
3/4 c. boiling water
1 tsp. instant coffee
1/2 c. part-skim Ricotta
  cheese
1/2 c. skim milk
3 TB. cocoa
1 pinch salt
6 TB. sugar

In blender, combine egg, gelatin, and cold water, processing for 10 seconds. Scrape mixture down and blend 10 more seconds. Let mixture stand about 1 minute or until gelatin softens. Add boiling water and blend 10 seconds. Add coffee, cheese, milk, cocoa, salt, and sugar. Blend until smooth, about 1 minute. Pour into 4 dessert glasses and chill 2 hours.

Calories per serving: 168
Fat: 5 gm. Cholesterol: 69 mg.
Sodium: 91 mg.
For exchange diets, count: 1 fruit, 1 fat

Preparation time: 2 1/2 hours

Speed Alert: Recipe requires 2 1/2 hours.

COFFEE BARS
YIELD: 24 BARS

★ ★ ★

1/2 c. margarine
1 c. brown sugar
1 egg or 1/4 c. liquid egg
   substitute
1 tsp. almond extract
1 tsp. vanilla
1 2/3 c. flour
1 TB. instant coffee powder
1/4 tsp. salt
1/2 tsp. baking soda
1/2 tsp. baking powder
1/2 tsp. cinnamon
1/2 tsp. nutmeg
1/2 c. hot water
1/2 c. raisins
1/2 c. walnuts
Powdered sugar

Preheat oven to 350° F. Cream margarine and sugar. Beat in egg, almond, and vanilla. Combine dry ingredients in a separate bowl and add alternately with hot water. Fold in raisins and nuts. Spread batter in a 10 x 15-inch pan that has been sprayed with nonstick cooking spray. Bake for 20 minutes. Bars are done when they are evenly lightly browned. Cool and dust with powdered sugar before cutting and serving.

Calories per 1-bar serving: 128
Fat: 5 gm. Cholesterol: 11 mg. with egg, 0 with substitute
Sodium: 97 mg.
For exchange diets, count: 1 bread/starch, 1 fat

Preparation time: 45 min.

FRESH FRUIT SOUP
YIELD: 8 1-C. SERVINGS

★ ★ ★

3 TB. minute tapioca

2 TB. sugar or equivalent
sugar substitute

1 c. water

6 oz. frozen orange juice
concentrate

16 oz. frozen strawberries
without sugar

1 small can mandarin
oranges

Combine tapioca, sugar, and water in a saucepan and allow to stand for 5 minutes. Then cook until clear. (If using sugar substitute, add to tapioca after cooking.) Add orange juice, strawberries, and oranges. Chill for 30 minutes. This dessert keeps well covered and refrigerated for 3 days.

Calories per 1-c. serving: 132
Fat: less than 1 gm. Cholesterol: 0
Sodium: 4 mg.
For exchange diets, count: 2 fruit

Preparation time: 45 min.

FRUIT CRUNCH FOR ICE MILK AND SHERBET
YIELD: 8 SERVINGS, 2 TB. EACH

★ ★ ★

1 c. wheat germ
2 TB. sugar
1/2 tsp. cinnamon
1 TB. margarine
1 TB. grated orange or lemon
   rind

Preheat oven to 200° F. Melt margarine and pour in bottom of a pie pan. Add wheat germ, sugar, cinnamon, and fruit peeling. Mix well, and bake for 45 minutes, stirring twice during baking. Store cooled crunch mix in a covered container. Serve over sherbet or ice milk.

Calories per 2 TB. serving: 78
Fat: 3 gm. Cholesterol: 0
Sodium: 17 mg.
For exchange diets, count: 1/2 bread/starch, 1/2 fat

Preparation time: 60 min.

FRUIT PLATE WITH STRAWBERRY DIP
YIELD: 4 1/2-C. SERVINGS

★ ★ ★

1 1/2 c. low-fat cottage cheese

1/3 c. sugar or equivalent
sugar substitute

1 tsp. almond flavoring

1/2 c. diced strawberries,
drained

Assorted fruits for dipping
such as: chunks of
pineapple or bananas,
wedges of peaches, apples,
kiwi fruit, or pears.

Combine cottage cheese, sugar or substitute, almond, and berries in a blender. Process until smooth. Transfer to a small, pretty serving bowl and place on a large plate with fruit around the bowl.

Calories per 1/2-c. serving of dip: 150 with sugar; 86 with substitute
Fat: 2 gm. Cholesterol: 7 mg.
Sodium: 344 mg.
For exchange diets, count: 1/2 fruit, 1 1/2 skim milk (with sugar)
With substitute: 1/2 skim milk, 1/2 fruit

Preparation time: 20 min.

KIWI FOR COMPANY
YIELD: 8 1-C. SERVINGS

★ ★ ★

6 kiwi fruits, peeled and
  sliced
8 oz. pineapple chunks, in
  juice
3 bananas, sliced diagonally

Dressing:
1 1/2 tsp. grated orange peel
1/2 tsp. ginger
1 c. nonfat yogurt
1/4 c. light mayonnaise
2 TB. honey

In a large salad bowl, gently mix kiwi fruit, pineapple and juice,
bananas, and grapes. Cover and refrigerate for 20 minutes,
allowing flavors to blend. Combine ingredients for dressing with
a whisk in a small mixing bowl. Pour dressing over fruits just
before serving. This dessert can be used as a leftover for up to 48
hours.

Calories per 1-c. serving: 153
Fat: 3 gm. Cholesterol: 3 mg.
Sodium: 45 mg.
For exchange diets, count: 2 fruit, 1 fat

Preparation time: 30 min.

LEMON CITRON CRISPS
YIELD: 72 COOKIES

★ ★ ★

3 c. flour
2 tsp. baking powder
2 TB. cinnamon
1 tsp. ground cloves
1/2 tsp. nutmeg
1 c. thinly sliced citron
Grated peel of 1 lemon
2 c. sugar
4 eggs or 1 c. liquid egg
  substitute

Sift all dry ingredients together. Stir in citron and lemon peel and set aside. Using an electric mixer and a large mixing bowl, beat eggs or substitute and sugar together until very thick. Fold in dry ingredients and citron and lemon peel. Chill dough 30 minutes. Preheat oven to 350° F. Roll out dough on floured board. Cut into 72 2-inch squares or Christmas shapes. Bake on greased cookie sheet for 15 minutes. These cookies freeze well. The dough can also be refrigerated for up to 10 days and baked as needed.

Calories per cookie: 51
Fat: less than 1 gm.
Cholesterol: 20 mg. with egg; 0 with substitute
Sodium: 14 mg.
For exchange diets, count: 1/2 bread/starch

Preparation time: 45 min.

LIME CHEESECAKE
YIELD: 8 SLICES

* * *

> 1/2 c. crushed salt-free
>   pretzels
> 1 TB. margarine
> 3 c. low-fat (1% fat) cottage
>   cheese
> 1/2 c. sugar
> 3 TB. flour
> 2 eggs, beaten or 1/2 c. liquid
>   egg substitute
> 1/2 c. skim milk
> 2 TB. lime juice
> 1 TB. finely grated lime peel

Preheat oven to 350° F. Spray a 9-inch pie pan with nonstick cooking spray. Combine pretzels and margarine in a bowl and press into the pie pan. Bake for 2 minutes at 350° F. Leave the oven on. Cool the crust. In a blender or food processor, process cottage cheese smooth. Add sugar and flour, continuing to blend smooth. Add eggs or substitute, slowly blending in and scraping the sides of the container with a spatula. Add milk, lime juice, and rind, processing just until blended. Slowly pour cheese mixture into the crust. Bake for 45 minutes at 350° F. or until toothpick inserted in center comes out clean. Cool, then refrigerate until serving time.

Calories per 1-slice serving: 210 with sugar; 167 with substitute
Fat: 4 gm.   Cholesterol: 48 mg. with eggs; 4 mg. with substitute
Sodium: 390 mg.
For exchange diets, count: 1 skim milk, 1 bread/starch, 1 fat
With sugar substitute, count: 1 skim milk, 1/2 bread/starch, 1 fat

Preparation time: 2 hours

Speed Alert: This dessert should be chilled for at least 1 hour after baking.

MARINATED FRUIT ON A PLATTER
YIELD: 8 SERVINGS

★ ★ ★

1 firm banana, peeled and cut
   in 1 1/2-inch chunks

1 golden delicious apple,
   quartered

1 red delicious apple,
   quartered

1 Granny Smith apple,
   quartered

4 pineapple rings

2 fresh oranges, peeled and
   sliced into rings

1 kiwi fruit, peeled and sliced

Poppy seed garnish

Marinade:

1 c. white wine

1 TB. grenadine

1 can sugar-free 7 Up®

2 TB. lemon juice

1/2 c. pineapple juice

Combine ingredients for marinade in a 2-qt. bowl. Add prepared fruit, cover, and refrigerate for 1/2 to 1 1/2 hours. Remove fruit to a platter and sprinkle with poppy seeds.

Calories per 3/4-c. serving: 60
Fat: 0 Cholesterol: 0
Sodium: 25 mg.
For exchange diets, count: 1 fruit

Preparation time: 45 min.

OATMEAL CRUNCH APPLE CRISP
YIELD: 12 1/2-C. SERVINGS

★ ★ ★

8 medium apples suited for
   baking, such as McIntosh,
   Rome or Jonathans
1 TB. lemon juice

Topping:
1/4 c. oatmeal
1 c. bran flakes, crushed fine
1/2 c. brown sugar
1/3 c. whole wheat flour
1/3 c. margarine
2 tsp. cinnamon

Preheat oven to 375° F. Core and finely slice apples into an 8 x
11-inch baking dish. Sprinkle with lemon juice. Combine
ingredients for topping in a 1-quart bowl, using a pastry cutter to
make a crumbly mixture. Sprinkle the topping over apples.
Bake for 45 minutes or MICROWAVE for 18 to 22 minutes until
apples are tender.

Calories per 1/2-c. serving: 158
Fat: 6 gm. Cholesterol: 0
Sodium: 69 mg.
For exchange diets, count: 1 fruit, 1 fat, 1 bread/starch

Preparation time: 45 min.

PEAR MELBA DESSERT
YIELD: 4 SERVINGS

★ ★ ★

> 4 ripe pears
> Lemon juice
> 3 oz. reduced-calorie cream
>   cheese
> 2 TB. almonds
> 10-oz. package frozen
>   raspberries
> 2 TB. sugar or equivalent
>   sugar substitute
> 1 TB. cornstarch
> 1/4 c. red wine

Halve and core pears. Peel, if desired. Brush the exposed pear flesh with lemon juice. Arrange 2 pear halves on dessert plates or all of the pear halves on a large serving platter. Shape well-chilled cheese into 8 balls and dip in almonds. Place the cheese balls, almond side up in the center of the pear halves, then refrigerate. Combine all remaining ingredients in a saucepan and cook until clear, whisking thick. Serve warm over stuffed pears.

Calories per 2 pear halves: 188
Fat: 8 gm. Cholesterol: 16 mg.
Sodium: 86 mg.
For exchange diets, count: 1 fruit, 1 1/2 fat, 1 bread/starch

Preparation time: 30 min.

PERFECT RASPBERRY CHIFFON
YIELD: 8 1/2-C. SERVINGS

★ ★ ★

> 1 10-oz. pkg. sweetened
>   frozen raspberries
> 1 TB. unflavored gelatin
> 1/2 c. water, lukewarm
> 6 TB. sugar
> 1 TB. flour
> 3 TB. lemon juice
> 1/3 c. ice water
> 1/3 c. nonfat dry milk powder

Thaw berries and drain, reserving juice and saving 8 firm berries
for garnish. Soften gelatin in water. In a saucepan, combine
4 TB. sugar with flour. Add reserved raspberry juice and
softened gelatin. Stir and heat slowly until sugar is dissolved.
Remove from heat and add 2 TB. of the lemon juice and the
berries. Cook until thick and syrupy, but not set. Chill the
beaters of an electric mixer. In a chilled bowl, combine ice water
and milk powder. Beat until soft peaks form (3 to 4 minutes).
Add the remaining tablespoon of lemon juice and beat another 3
to 4 minutes until stiff. Fold in the remaining 2 TB. of sugar,
blending well at low speed. Fold mixture into raspberry gelatin.
Spoon into stemmed glasses, and chill 45 minutes or until firm,
garnishing each serving with reserved whole berry.

Calories per 1/2-c. serving: 97
Fat: less than 1 gm. Cholesterol: 1 mg.
Sodium: 28 mg.
For exchange diets, count: 1 1/2 fruit

Preparation time: 60 min.

PIE CRUST FOR ALL SEASONS
YIELD: 1 9-INCH CRUST, 8 SLICES

★ ★ ★

3 egg whites at room
  temperature
1 c. sugar
1 1/2 tsp. vanilla
14 squares soda crakers,
  rolled fine
1/2 tsp. baking soda
1/2 c. chopped walnuts

Preheat oven to 325° F. In a medium mixing bowl, beat egg whites until frothy. Gradually add sugar until stiff peaks form. Fold in vanilla, crackers, soda, and nuts. Spray a 9-inch pie pan with nonstick cooking spray and transfer egg white mixture to the pan, spreading evenly over the bottom and sides. Bake for 45 minutes. Cool to room temperature and fill with fruit filling or skim milk based puddings.

Calories per 1/8 crust: 143
Fat: 3 gm. Cholesterol: 0
Sodium: 129 mg.
For exchange diets, count: 2 bread/starches

Preparation time: 55 min.

PUMPKIN PIE
YIELD : 8 SERVINGS

★ ★ ★

Crust:

1 1/2 c. (use 24 squares)
  graham cracker crumbs
1 TB. sugar
1 TB. melted margarine

Filling:

1 c. soft tofu
1 1/2 c. solid pack pumpkin
1/2 c. sugar
2 TB. cornstarch
1/2 c. skim milk
1 egg or 1/4 c. liquid egg
  substitute
3 tsp. pumpkin pie spice
1/2 tsp. salt

Preheat oven to 400° F. Mix ingredients for crust together in a
9-inch pie plate, pressing evenly over the bottom and sides.
Combine all ingredients for the filling in a blender or food
processor until smooth. Pour into pie crust and bake for 50
minutes to 1 hour until set.

Calories per 1/8 pie: 221
Fat: 7 gm. Cholesterol: 34 mg. with egg; 0 with substitute
Sodium: 147 mg.
For exchange diets, count: 1 fruit, 1 fat,
1/2 skim milk, 1 bread/starch

Preparation time: 1 hr., 15 min.

ROLLED PUMPKIN CHEESECAKE
YIELD: 18 SLICES

★ ★ ★

3 eggs, slightly beaten or 3/4 c. liquid egg substitute	1 tsp. pumpkin pie spice
1 c. sugar	1/2 tsp. salt
2/3 c. canned pumpkin	
3/4 c. flour	*Filling:*
1 tsp. baking powder	1/2 c. powdered sugar
2 tsp. cinnamon	8 oz. ricotta cheese
	2 tsp. vanilla

Preheat oven to 350°F. Spray a 10 x 15-inch jelly-roll pan with nonstick cooking spray. Place a large sheet of wax paper over bottom and sides of pan. In a medium-sized mixing bowl, beat eggs until foamy. Gradually add sugar and pumpkin, mixing well. Sift dry ingredients, and gradually add to pumpkin mixture. Stir in walnuts. Pour batter into prepared pan and bake for 25 minutes, or until an inserted toothpick comes out clean. Cool for 45 minutes. Remove cake from pan, tear off wax paper, and roll cake in jelly roll fashion, covering with a towel. Meanwhile, strain liquid from the ricotta cheese by placing in a colander for 30 minutes. Using an electric mixer and a small mixing bowl, mix powdered sugar and vanilla into the curds of the ricotta cheese until smooth. Unroll cake and spread cheese mixture evenly over the cake. Re-roll in jelly-roll fashion and cover with plastic wrap. Refrigerate at least 1 1/2 hours before serving. Slice and serve.

Calories per slice: 148
Fat: 3 gm. Cholesterol: 50 mg.
Sodium: 29 mg.
For exchange diets, count: 1 1/2 bread/starch, 1/2 fat

Preparation time: 3 hours

Speed Alert: Recipe takes 3 hours.

SHARON B's WHOLE WHEAT APPLE CAKE
YIELD: 8 SERVINGS

★ ★ ★

A wonderful baker and my childhood friend, Sharon Buenger Holdiman, gave this recipe to me.

1/2 c. whole wheat flour
1/2 c. white flour
2 TB. wheat germ
1 tsp. soda
1/2 tsp. cinnamon
1/4 tsp. salt
1/4 tsp. nutmeg
2 c. finely chopped and peeled
  apples
1/4 c. sugar
1/3 c. brown sugar
1/4 c. vegetable oil
1/2 tsp. vanilla
1 egg or 1/4 c. liquid egg
  substitute

Preheat oven to 350° F. Mix dry ingredients together in a small bowl. Set aside. In a medium-sized bowl, cream sugars and oil. Stir in apples and vanilla. Fold in dry ingredients. Pour into an 8-inch square pan that has been sprayed with nonstick cooking spray. Bake for 30 minutes until golden brown. Dust with powdered sugar when cool. Serve with vanilla ice milk.

Calories per serving of cake only: 214
Fat: 8 gm. Cholesterol: 32 mg. with egg; 0 with substitute
Sodium: 174 mg.
For exchange diets, count: 2 bread/starch, 1 1/2 fat

Preparation time: 60 min.

AUTHOR BIOGRAPHY

M.J. Smith, M.A., R.D. /L.D. is President of Menu Management Incorporated, a business that provides nutrition services to health care agencies, publishers, and food companies. She is the former editor of *Menu Management.*

Ms. Smith earned a B.S. from Eastern Illinois University and completed her M.A. and Dietetic Internship at the University of Iowa. She has had 12 years experience counseling individuals in diet management, and has served on the faculties of the University of Northern Iowa and Clarke College. In addition to management responsibilities in health care organizations, Ms. Smith is the founder of Nutri-Shop, a supermarket program. She has held many positions within professional dietetic organizations and is currently the Media Representative for the Iowa Dietetic Association. She provides commentary on nutrition issues for the *Des Moines Register.*

Ms. Smith lives in Guttenberg, Iowa, a Mississippi River community, with her husband Dr. Andrew Smith, a family physician, and her two children, Frederic and Elizabeth. Her interests include low-fat cooking, gardening, and politics. She is an avid walker.

BIBLIOGRAPHY

American Heart Association Diet, An Eating Plan for Healthy Americans. Dallas: American Heart Association. 1988.

American Dietetic Association, Manual of Clinical Dietetics. Chicago: American Dietetic Association. 1989.

Diet, Nutrition and Cancer Prevention: The Good News. National Institutes of Health, U.S. Department of Health and Human Services. 1987.

Franz, Marion. *Fast Food Facts*. Minneapolis: Diabetes Center Inc. 1987.

Netzer, Corrine. *The Complete Book of Food Counts*. New York: Dell Publishing. 1988.

Pennington, Jean and Church, Helen. *Food Values*. New York: Harper and Row. 1980.

United States Department of Agriculture. *Cholesterol Content of Eggs*. 1989.

INDEX

★ ★ ★